WELLINGTON AT WALMER

WELLINGTON AT WALMER

Gregory Holyoake

Buckland Publications Ltd
Barwick Road, Dover

DEDICATION:

To MISS DORIS SALTER

curator of

The Salter Collection
of Period Costume at Deal

'in admiration'

Published in 1996 by Buckland Publications Ltd
Barwick Road, Dover, Kent CT17 0LG

*Silhouette on title page reproduced by kind permission of
Mary Evans Picture Library*

*Frontispiece – A bronze of the Duke of Wellington framed in a window arch
overlooking Walmer Castle gardens (photograph by Gregory Holyoake)*

ISBN 07212 0970 X

Printed in England by Buckland Press Ltd, Barwick Road, Dover CT17 0LG
and 125 High Holborn, London WC1V 6QA

CONTENTS

Sir Arthur Wellesley, first Duke of Wellington

ILLUSTRATIONS

FOREWORD

FOR ALMOST a quarter of a century (1829-1852) the Duke of Wellington in his role as Lord Warden of the Cinque Ports resided for one third of every year at Walmer Castle on the coast of Kent and it was there that he died in 1852.

The Duke took great pleasure in his 'charming marine residence' and he welcomed a host of distinguished visitors including Queen Victoria and Prince Albert who spent an invigorating seaside holiday there in the autumn of 1842.

This book explores the private life of the Iron Duke and highlights many intriguing aspects of his complicated personality including his love of field sports, devotion to religion, concern for defence, attitude to health and perhaps most surprisingly his inordinate fondness for children.

Although he lived a Spartan regime at Walmer Castle, he was a warm, generous host and his active concern for his neighbours endeared him to the local community.

Yet all the time he paced the ramparts overlooking the English Channel to keep an ever-watchful eye on his old arch enemy – France.

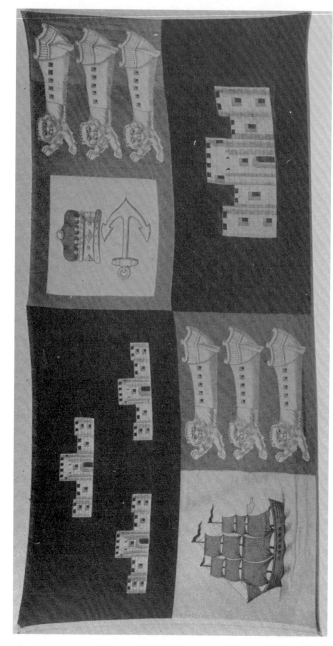

The Lord Warden's Flag (photo by Ray Warner)

Chapter One

SIR ARTHUR WELLESLEY AT DEAL

THE WARDENSHIP of the Cinque Ports fell vacant on the death of Lord Liverpool on 4 December 1828. This office had been held by three Prime Ministers in succession and, as Arthur Wellesley, first Duke of Wellington, was Prime Minister at the time when the vacancy occurred, to him it was inevitably offered.

In a letter to King George IV, the Duke had already expressed his willingness to take up the office since it was 'of great influence and power but without any salary' as the substantial salary had ceased upon the demise of the previous Lord Warden. On 20 January 1829 the Iron Duke, then in his sixtieth year, was duly installed as Constable of Dover Castle and Lord Warden and Admiral of the Cinque Ports. It was entirely characteristic that he assumed office without any of the traditional ceremonies.

Since Lionel Sackville, first Duke of Dorset, took up residence in 1708, Walmer Castle has been the official home of the Lords Warden of the Cinque Ports and so for the remaining twenty-three years of his life the Duke of Wellington also made it one of his three homes. His other residences were Stratfield Saye in Hampshire and Apsley House known as 'No.1, London'. Immediately after the prorogation of Parliament the Duke would travel down to Walmer in the early autumn where he would remain until the first or second week in November.

This journey he accomplished, without fail, annually. Initially he travelled by road (the Duke had an abhorrence of trains after witnessing an horrific accident at the opening of the London to Manchester line in 1830) until the impossibility of finding relays of horses along the neglected lanes of Kent forced him much against his will to cease from posting.

Whenever the Duke was in residence at Walmer Castle an enormous flag was flown from the tower. Invariably, this was the Union Jack since the castle was still regarded as a royal residence. True, the Lord Warden had a flag – a gorgeous affair of azure, crimson and gold featuring the four castles of his coast. a sailing ship, an anchor surmounted by a ducal coronet and three lions dimidiated with the sterns of ships – but this was only flown at sea.

11

Early Victorian engraving of Walmer Castle by George Shepherd

Since the Duke did not own a yacht, he never flew his flag. Indeed, it would appear that the custom of flying the Lord Warden's flag eventually fell into disuse for when a later Lord Warden, W. H. Smith, flew the flag from the foremast of his yacht, *Pandora*, in the Downs, that anchorage of water off Deal, it caused considerable confusion to shipping!

The Duke of Wellington's response to his fortress home was ecstatic. 'This place is delightful, very well furnished; and in a tolerable state of repair for this summer,' he wrote to his friend, Mrs Harriet Arbuthnot, on 13 July 1829. He was heartily welcomed by his neighbours because of his kindness and concern for poorer folk and his courtesy and lack of formality towards the nobility.

Abundant stories are told to illustrate his amiability. He once strolled boldly into a Deal lodging-house in order to invite a total stranger to shoot his woodcock and when a neighbour complained of the devastation caused by the castle rooks he meekly replied that they would be destroyed. He attended balls at the local Assembly Rooms; went on shopping sprees to Dover; enjoyed sea bathing from the beach at Walmer; took visitors to chat with an elderly woman who lived in an upturned boat near the castle and rode over uninvited to converse with the miller at Ripple Mill. He did not even baulk when the parish authorities ruled that, since Walmer Castle had now lost its military aspect, the Duke was eligible to pay domestic rates on his new home. After all, he agreed cheerfully, the money would contribute towards 'Relief of the Poor'.

There is little record of his presence at Walmer during his first year of Wardenship. He certainly came down, however, for on 31 August he appointed William Denne to be 'one of the warreners and game-keepers within the Warren of Dover Castle'. More importantly, he reaffirmed the appointment of George Leith as Captain of Walmer Castle and elected Edward Thompson to be his Lieutenant.

Yet it was not all pleasure for the Duke at Walmer. At this time the office of Lord Warden was an important and arduous one. His duties were numerous and varied: he daily countersigned the orders of the garrison of regular troops at Dover; he consigned Cinque Ports debtors to a special jail on the roadway leading to Dover Castle; he supervised the various harbour works, lifeboats and salvage; he was responsible for the defence of the Channel; he appointed and regulated local magistrates; he collected droits of Admiralty (fees and rights to the proceeds of seizures, wrecks, etc) and, above all, provided competent pilots for the navigation of the English Channel. Into all these concerns the Duke threw himself whole-heartedly.

Characteristically, he refused any payment to himself and the profits of his office, which amounted to £2,973 12s 6d in his first year, were returned into public funds.

*

Every year the Duke presided over the Court of Lode-Manage at Dover, often travelling down specially from London or even Stratfield Saye. This ancient assembly met to appoint and discipline Channel pilots and was an occasion for pomp and circumstance.

The author of *Dover: Reminiscences of an Ancient Freeman* describes these impressive gatherings: 'The Duke's Court of Lode-Manage used to be opened in St James' Church. The Duke and pilots walked in procession – the Duke in a blue coat and red collar, the pilots in blue coats, gilt buttons and primrose waistcoats; and after the court was opened behind the communion table the

The Port of Deal at the time of the Napoleonic Wars

Master of the Fellowship was elected by open vote. The procession reformed and walked to the Old Antwerp Hotel on the Market Place for the despatch of business.' The last Court of Lode-Manage was held on 21 October 1851 – the year before the Duke's demise – after which the responsibility for the regulation of Channel pilots passed to the Master and Brethren of Trinity House, Deptford. Soon the role of Lord Warden, which the Duke had taken up solely for the purpose of public service, became one of his principal interests and delights.

Certainly, his life style was now in direct contrast to the period at the beginning of the nineteenth century when Sir Arthur Wellesley, then a young officer in the British Army, had frequented the district during the Napoleonic Wars. . .

14

After the Battle of Trafalgar in 1805 when Nelson defeated Napoleon at sea, it was left to Wellington to pursue the Emperor on land. Already, as a colonel in command of the 33rd Foot, Arthur Wellesley had distinguished himself in India at the Battle of Assaye in 1803.

When he returned to England, his ship, HMS *Trident*, dropped anchor in the Downs and he stepped ashore at Deal after an absence from this country of nine years. Confusion reigned all about him. He was highly amused when a certain officer at Deal desired Wellesley to wait upon him and gave him some direction to which Sir Arthur replied: 'The order shall be attended to, but I rather believe you will find that I am your senior officer instead of you being mine.' And so it proved to be!

From his return in September 1805 until his departure as a major-general in charge of an expeditionary force to Portugal in July 1808, which marked the commencement of the Peninsular Wars, there was an anxious time of waiting in which the now forty-years old soldier was conscious that his talents were not being fully exploited. During this period of comparative inactivity, Sir Arthur Wellesley was often at Deal.

*

When Bonaparte marched to combat the united forces of Austria and Russia in 1805, the British Government resolved to create a favourable diversion by sending an auxiliary force into northern Germany in an attempt to reconquer Hanover, of which British monarchs from George I to William IV were also king. A considerable force of 13,000 men was assembled in the Downs under the command of Lord Cathcart in the closing months of that year and set sail under the temporary orders of General Don. Sir Arthur Wellesley was appointed to the command of a brigade in this army and he embarked from Deal in late December. Three times he attempted to sail but he was driven back by storms losing each time two or three hundred men by shipwreck on the Goodwin Sands. After a week at sea, he landed near Bremen where news of the Battle of Austerlitz, in which Napoleon had crushed the Austro-Russian army, filtered through and it was thought prudent to withdraw the English force. Thus, Wellesley returned to England without firing a single shot!

The crossing to Germany had not been without humour. A ten gun brig had conveyed Wellesley to join Lord Cathcart. The captain had his wife on board, and the main cabin was divided only by a flag – the couple on one side, Sir Arthur on the other. During the voyage the lady did not once leave her cabin but when the vessel was coming to anchor at Cuxhaven, Wellesley heard her order the cabin boy, who was acting as her maid, to bring her the captain's comb and toothbrush and a pair of stockings as she was going ashore!

*Catherine 'Kitty' Pakenham, first Duchess of Wellington
(Mary Evans Picture Library)*

During 1806 Sir Arthur Wellesley was posted to Hastings in command of 'a few troops' (February); was elected MP for Rye (April) and married Catherine 'Kitty' Pakenham in Dublin (April). Courtship had lasted an ominous thirteen years and had to be abandoned temporarily by Arthur through penury prior to his campaign in India. Theirs was an ill-starred union, doomed to failure almost from the start, though she bore him two sons. Kitty was unable to match the speed of his ascent and her timorous, intellectually limited character grated on her husband constantly so that their moments of happiness were few and far between.

The end of summer saw Wellesley back in Hastings in his military command. He was still there in October and starting to chafe a bit at not being sent overseas. 'Another of my regiments has received orders to march to Deal where I suppose it is to embark for the Continent,' he complained bitterly to his eldest brother, Richard Wellesley, who had succeeded to their father's Irish Earldom of Mornington in 1781. 'I hope that as four out of five regiments have now been taken from my command to be sent on service, I shall now be sent; and I don't care in what situation, I am only afraid that Lord Greville does not understand that I don't want a chief command if it cannot be given to me; and that I should be very sorry to stay at home when others go abroad, only because I cannot be commander in chief.'

His wish was not at that time granted and so he followed his troops to Deal. Here the bustling activity only served to contrast his impotency. Presumably this was the period when he rented the modest residence, 'a dwelling of the better class', a little way along Castle Road, Upper Walmer. Nowadays, this is known as 'Wellesley House' or sometimes simply 'The Duke's House'. A plaque affixed to the wall states that: 'Lieutenant-General Sir Arthur Wellesley lived here before leaving for the Peninsular Campaign in 1808.'

The Duke's house in Castle Road, Walmer

17

The earliest surviving letter written to Kitty by Arthur after their marriage was written from this house at Deal. It marks the tip of the iceberg floating towards the union of this mis-matched couple – for Kitty had already begun to mismanage household affairs:

Deal, December 6th 1806

My dearest Kitty,

I send underneath, an order for 50 Pounds; but I wish you would not send it till you want the Money as the Bankers will not have it in their hands, till they have disposed of some stock of mine. George [an unidentified manservant] is to have 14 shillings a week Board Wages, and if he should want more, or not be satisfied, give him warning; for it is time to draw a line.

Ever Yours most affectionately,

A.W.

Gradually, the troops, who had been billeted in the various taverns and lodging houses at Deal, began to leave for Ireland, via Liverpool. There they would be under the command of Sir Arthur Wellesley, newly-created lieutenant-general, on his first expedition to Portugal in 1808.

*

At the time that her husband was becoming entangled with the war in Spain and Portugal, Kitty Wellesley took a holiday. Following the advice of her doctor, she brought her two sons, Arthur and Charles, to Broadstairs where she thought the invigorating Channel breezes might do them a power of good.

Her visit coincided with the embarkation of the ill-conceived Walcheren expedition which set sail from the Downs during the summer of 1809. The object of the mission, which was under the doubtful leadership of the Earl of Chatham (the eldest son of Pitt the Elder who was prime minister in the mid 1700s, and elder brother of Pitt the Younger who was prime minister for twenty years at the end of that century), was an attack upon the low-lying island of Walcheren, Flushing and other arsenals in Holland.

The expedition was of such magnitude that it is difficult now to imagine. A fleet of several hundred men-of-war was stationed in the Channel waters with transports employed for many weeks embarking troops from the beaches at Deal and Walmer as soon as they arrived. Independent of these warships engaged in the outfit of aggression were numerous ships at anchor detained for want of convoys – so that the whole of the Downs between the North and South Forelands was one great mass of shipping. In its initial stages, the expedition

Sailing ships in the Downs

was regarded in the nature of a holiday particularly by the gentry who had gathered on the beach at Deal to witness the colourful sight presented in the Downs. Hundreds of soldiers and sailors stood at the water's edge waiting for boats to convey them to their ships while scores of women crowded on the shore to take a final leave of their menfolk before they sailed for battle. Naturally, the local boatmen reaped a rich reward, their boats requisitioned for fetching and carrying all manner of goods both day and night; and the town itself was filled to overflowing with strangers who had come on some errand or other from all parts of the British Isles.

On 21 July Kitty Wellesley travelled down to Deal to join the throng and gaze upon the immense shipping still in the Channel. 'A more magnificent [sight] cannot be conceived than that of the Fleet now in the Downs, above 500 sail of transports including 50 men-of-war. God Almighty protect our brave Men, success attend them.'

*

General Nugent toured his battalions along the Kent coast that fateful summer. His American wife accompanied him, breathlessly recording minute details in her journal:

> 21st July – Went to Broadstairs, Kingsgate, & co, and then set off, in the evening for Deal. Met Lady Wellesley, & co there, and had a nice walk on the beach. The Downs full of ships, and the sight altogether magnificent. The poor fellows cheering as they embarked, and I don't know why, but I could scarcely refrain from shedding tears at their joy; it seemed, indeed, so thoughtless, when they were soon to meet an enemy, & co. But soldiers, I believe, never think, and perhaps it is fortunate that they do not.

General Nugent was actively concerned with an epidemic among his troops and travelled on his horse back and forth along the coast visiting the infirm. Dutifully he arranged suitable accommodation, medical care and, for those with no chance of recovery, a common grave. (The Archbishop of Canterbury obliged by consecrating a burial ground.) At times the general was hampered by privateers sweeping into the Downs and firing haphazardly at the shore. At that, Lady Nugent retorted, 'We were in a great fuss.'

Lady Nugent had duties of her own to perform. Her stay in Deal meant a constant round of supper parties, masked balls, musical concerts and carriage rides. Life, after all, must go on. . .

*

Yet another eyewitness was more specific concerning the nature of the Channel fleet: 'The land forces, commanded by the Earl of Chatham, were composed of forty thousand men, the flower of the British Army. This force was accompanied by a not less imposing naval force: thirty-nine sail of the line, three dozen frigates and innumerable satellites, bombships, gunboats, brigs, etc. which together with storeships, transports and other craft, amounted in the whole to upwards of 600 sail.'

The writer was twenty-years-old Captain Robert Blakeney, a member of the 28th Regiment of Foot, who later distinguished himself in the Peninsular Wars. In his autobiography he recalls the excitement of the concourse at Deal:

To join this splendid armament, the 28th Regiment marched from Colchester in the latter end of June, and reached Dover on July 4th. Thence we embarked on board frigates – a squadron of that class of men-of-war under command of Sir Richard Keats being destined to carry the reserve of the army. This arrangement was adopted in consequence of the frigates drawing less water than ships of the line, thus enabling them to be closer in shore and quicken the disembarkation of the reserve, who of course were the first troops to land.

We remained upwards of a week at Deal, awaiting final instructions and the junction of the whole. During this delay some thousand families, many of the highest lineage in the kingdom, visited Deal. All arrangements being finally terminated, this truly magnificent naval and military armament sailed on July 28th, 1809. Thousands of superbly dressed women crowded the beach; splendid equipages were numerous; all the musical bands in the fleet, as well as military and naval, joined in one general concert, playing the National Anthem, which, with the band and long-continued cheering on shore, enlivened the neighbourhood for miles around and caused the most enthusiastic excitement throughout the whole.

*

Yet another soldier who made up the thousands who passed before Kitty's eyes that fateful summer was Captain John Kincaid. As a lad of twenty-two years of age he joined as a volunteer the Second Battalion of the famous 95th, the immortal 'Rifles' in the Light Division. He had enlisted at Hythe Barracks in the spring of 1809 and a month later proceeded to form part of the expedition to Holland.

George Shepherd's engraving of Deal Castle showing its domesticated state with the Governor's lodging, a profusion of tall chimneys and the toll gate at the entrance to Walmer Strand

Captain Kincaid left this nervous, refreshingly honest account of his exploits:

With usual quixotic feelings of a youngster, I remember how desirous I was, on the march to Deal, to impress the minds of the natives with a suitable notion of the magnitude of my importance, by carrying a donkey load of pistols in my belt, and screwing my naturally placid countenance up to a pitch of ferocity beyond what it was calculated to bear.

We embarked in the Downs on board the *Hussar* frigate and afterwards removed to the *Namur*, a seventy-four, in which we were conveyed to our destination.

In spite of a cheerful temperament and a healthy constitution, Kincaid, like thousands of his fellow soldiers, fell a victim to the swamp-bred agues and fevers which destroyed that cursed expedition. Kitty Wellesley, in company with most of the gentility, was not around to see the vast numbers of sick and wounded soldiers returned to Deal in cramped boatloads that autumn. There, devoid of hope and care, they were left to die in their hundreds on the beaches at Deal and Walmer, no one able or willing to offer them shelter or sustenance.

As for Captain Kincaid, he was one of the lucky ones who lived to fight another day sharing in the glories of Wellington's victory at Waterloo. . .

*

Prior to Waterloo, Sir Arthur Wellesley, recently created Duke of Wellington, was again in Deal for part of August 1814 on his way to Paris having been appointed ambassador to France. Lord William Pitt Lennox, then aged fourteen, a son of the Duke and Duchess of Richmond, had been appointed an apprentice ADC to Wellington and accompanied him on his mission to the court of France. He recorded his excursion from London, travelling by carriage to Dover on 7 August.

At three o'clock, a salute from the batteries announced the arrival of Wellington at Dover. He alighted at Wright's Hotel and Ship Inn, and partook of some refreshment, but finding that the wind was blowing very fresh from the west-south-west, and the weather too rough to embark at that port, His Grace proceeded to Deal, about five o'clock. Vice-Admiral Foley preceded the Duke about an hour, in order to give the necessary directions for his reception on board the *Griffon*, sloop of war, to Captain Hewson.

Sandown Castle, the third of Henry VIII's fortifications built to protect the Downs, succumbed to the sea in the nineteenth century

22

Upon reaching Deal, where His Grace was received by all ranks with every demonstration of joy and respect, we found the Vice-Admiral in waiting; and accompanied by that gallant officer, and a great concourse of inhabitants, we proceeded to the boat prepared to take us off to the ship. Here again the Duke was heartily cheered. No sooner were we on board the *Griffon* than she got under way; and, with a strong wind, steered for Ostend.

Here follows the record from the log of the ship in which the Duke of Wellington and his suite embarked to illustrate what occurred on their crossing:

H.M.S. *Griffon*
Monday August 8th 1814

A.M. Strong winds and squally weather; at 9 weighed, and made sail under the courses and close reef topsails; at noon, strong gales and clear weather. P.M. Wind WSW; strong gales and cloudy; at 2.30, bore up; at 3.30, sent the gig on shore to Dover; at 5, gig returned, filled and made sail for the Downs: at 5.30, shortened sail, and came to, (small bower), Walmer Mill, on the west end of the hospital; at 6, answered telegraph made by *Monmouth*; at 6.20, embarked the Duke of Wellington and suite for Ostend, fired a salute of fifteen guns; at 7.30, weighed and made sail; at 9, North Foreland Light, N.W., North Sandhead Light, S by W; at 12, fresh gales and clear.

The Duke of Wellington never fell easily into the role of an ambassador for his relationship with the Continent, even after overwhelming victory, was for ever 'squally'. When Lord Warden he was occasionally cast in that self-same role but his suspicions of the French were lifelong and he stubbornly refused to believe that a country which was once our enemy could ever be an ally.

Field Marshal the Duke of Wellington

Chapter Two

LORD WARDEN OF THE CINQUE PORTS

TIME HAD made civilians of both the Duke and the seaside castle of which he had become master. Now the gunports were bedroom windows; its ramparts turned into verandahs while the moat was converted into the peaceful office of a kitchen garden. Walmer Castle still had its garrison, however, and during his Wardenship a sentry armed with a halberd kept guard at the main gate. Yet the alarm bell in the tower was only ever rung to summon folk to dinner!

Even the cannon – eight smooth-bore thirty-two pounders on the upper ramparts and six six-pounders on the lower, each bearing the royal cipher (*Georgius III Rex*) pointing seawards – remained silent. The castle was still officially a royal saluting station so once a year these guns were fired on the sovereign's birthday. Alarmingly, no-one showed concern that gunpowder was now stored in a magazine immediately beneath the kitchen stove!

During his occupation the Duke hardly altered the castle. True, he did install a hot water pipe system and introduced sash windows in an endeavour to cope with draughts. But he declined to put up a suspension bridge from the living rooms on to the beach (as did a later resident, Lord Granville) preferring to walk round by the drawbridge on the north side of the castle. The Duke had no knowledge of farming and therefore showed little interest in the management of the estate attached to the castle, yet everything else he oversaw carefully, punctiliously paying his bills himself week by week.

He was surrounded by old retainers: Kendall, his valet, had been with him for many years; Collins, the butler, even longer. His housekeeper, Mrs Norman, was followed by Mrs Allen who remained in office under two succeeding Lords Warden. She amassed a small fortune from escorting visitors around the castle in the Duke's absence although he constantly protested that the public were far too insistent in 'making a shew' of his bedroom and dressing room. Townsend, who acted as both warder and steward, had been a sergeant of the Grenadiers in the crowning charge of Waterloo.

Timbs, who visited the castle shortly after the Duke's death, left a detailed description of the interior:

The Castle . . . consists of a large central round tower surrounded by an inner wall of considerable strength. Most of the rooms are small, and some very unsystematically proportioned; they are connected by long, narrow and circuitous passages, the whole being kept scrupulously neat; while in some of those open to the air, plants and flowering shrubs are ranged along the walls, blooming amid the moss-grown and crumbling battlements.

The furniture of the castle is very plain and the walls of the principal rooms newly decorated with a few prints left by the previous Lords Warden. The unmistakable military character of the Duke is evident in the notices placed on many of the doors: 'SHUT THIS DOOR'. The Duke . . . occupied only one room, which was his study and bedchamber, and known as 'The Duke's Room'. It is in one of the smaller towers, of moderate size and was plainly furnished, methodically arranged, something like an officer's room in a garrison.

The Duke's study is a curiously irregular shaped room on the south side of the castle. Even in daytime it appears slightly gloomy despite sharp cross-lights from the two arched windows in the deep embrasures: one overlooking the celebrated gardens, the other commanding a dramatic view of the English Channel.

While residing at Walmer Castle, the Duke worked and slept in only one apartment, known as 'The Duke's Room'. Here can be seen his military camp bed and the high-backed chair in which he died

The Duke attempted a little cheer with bright furnishings. His original yellow moreen curtains, with their tattered tassels, and faded wallpaper, an oppressive trellis pattern, remained until recently. The carpet, though, is reproduction.

All the furniture is original. A handsome mahogany desk with a prop-up leather covered top and numerous drawers, some containing secret compartments, was built by the Duke's house carpenter at Stratfield Saye. Originally it stood in the recess, its surface ink-stained and littered with papers, facing seawards where it caught the morning sun. The Duke preferred to work standing up. An alternative writing desk has a single central stand, a side drawer and flaps for holding an inkwell and a candlestick. In the centre of the room is a high backed winged armchair, with its original faded yellow striped chintz cover, in which the Duke died.

Along one side of the room is the narrow folding camp-bed with criss-cross brass legs, silk headboard, wafer thin horsehair mattress and chamois leather pillow. Gleig asserts this was designed by the Duke to accompany him on his expedition to Russia in 1826. Its precise measurements are 6 feet 6 inches long by 2 feet 9 inches wide and it was so constructed that it could be folded up and packed away in a small compass.

Summer or winter, the tiny bedstead was without curtains and a single blanket with a 'blueish-green shot silk' quilt the only coverings, although an old military cloak was placed near to hand should the night prove exceptionally chilly. When one of his female admirers, Lady Mary Salisbury, expressed surprise that he should continue to make use of a bed in which there was no room to turn, the Duke's classic remark was: 'When it's time to turn over, it's time to turn out.'

This metal camp-bed features in a caricature by William Heath in 1829. The Duke is portrayed carrying the camp-bed complete with a canopy on his shoulders as he marches from Walmer Castle to Downing Street. Perspiration pours from his brow. The cartoon is entitled: 'Take Up Your Bed – and Walk!!!' and was intended to convey a general desire for the Duke to resign as Prime Minister. This satirical print informs us erroneously that 'this highly prized article of furniture' was regularly conveyed between Walmer Castle and Downing Street. When Prime Minister, the Duke resided at Apsley House (his servants occupied Downing Street) where he used a comfortable bed. At

*A satirical print featuring the famous military campbed in which the Duke
slept at Walmer: Take Up Your Bed and Walk!!!
(The Victoria and Albert Museum)*

Stratfield Saye the Duke slept on a sofa.

Bookshelves covered almost an entire wall of the Duke's room so that reading material was near to hand: histories, biographies, French memoirs, military reports, official publications, Parliamentary papers, the Bible, prayer book, Jeremy Taylor's *Holy Living and Dying* and Caesar's *Commentaries* – all well-thumbed.

Twin doors on either side of the bookcase concealed washing facilities: two bronze shaving mugs, a ewer and basin in common blue and white floral patterned china. A deal washstand with a swivel mirror on a tall stand, a simple towel horse, a chest of drawers, needlework firescreens and one or two chairs comprised the rest of the Duke's furniture.

On the walls hung a few common engravings including a portrait of the tragic actress, Sarah Siddons. Pride of place, eventually, went to a portrait of the Duke's godson, Prince Arthur (1850-1942), the seventh child of Queen Victoria and Prince Albert. Displayed on the mantelpiece below the chimney-glass were two ornaments, an ivory statuette of Napoleon and a figurine of Jenny Lind, the 'Swedish Nightingale' – a strange mixture of discord and harmony!

*

The Duke dressed as a civilian while at Walmer Castle. His clothes rarely altered – a blue frock coat, white waistcoat, white trousers, a low-crowned narrow-brimmed hat and a pure white cravat fastened with a silver buckle. Occasionally the colour of his waistcoat brightened to red or blue. He never wore a greatcoat but when out for his strolls along our breezy coast he often threw a cape about his shoulders.

His evening attire consisted of a blue coat with silver buttons, a white waistcoat and cravat, black breeches and silk stockings, or tight black pantaloons. Generally, he wore plain buckled shoes but when in the presence of officers only he preferred to don Wellington boots! On formal occasions he invariably dressed for dinner in the uniform of the Lord Warden.

*

The Duke was most anxious to share his new home with his many friends. Alas, he was not fortunate with his first few guests. Lady Lyndhurst, wife of the Lord Chancellor, miscarried in a carriage half-way up Dover Hill; Mrs Fox outstayed her welcome two days after her host had left remaining alone with Lord Chesterfield. Disgusted, the Duke vowed he would never allow her into any of his houses again!

His most intimate acquaintances were the Arbuthnots who were frequently at Walmer Castle. After a mixed career of Parliamentary service and diplomacy, the Right Honourable Charles Arbuthnot became Commissioner of Woods and

Forests. In 1814, being then a widower and close on fifty, he married a handsome and clever woman, Miss Harriet Fane.

Between Mrs Arbuthnot and the Duke an intimacy began which developed into a close and lasting friendship. The Duke always wore about his neck a locket with a portrait of Harriet fastened by a chain made from her hair and this was discovered on his body after his death. He was devastated when she died suddenly of cholera in August 1834. The Duke persuaded her widower to surrender his own house, 'Woodford', in Northamptonshire, in order to become his permanent companion and to share his three homes including Walmer Castle.

Charles Arbuthnot was described as 'a little old rosy-faced man'. All his friends called him 'Gosh'. The Duke and he were like brothers. Indeed, Raikes noticed how the two veterans were well-matched: 'Arbuthnot is his . . . second self, from which it seems he has no secrets hid. I observe that, at breakfast, he shows him almost all his letters, and his character is so mild and placid, that it blends admirably with the Duke, who, with all his fine qualities, when worried and vexed by his multifarious business, is subject at time to momentary fits of anger and excitement – sometimes visited upon Arbuthnot himself.'

Only two years of age divided them but Arbuthnot was not only the older but the weaker and the Duke realised this. He watched over his friend with a marked degree of tenderness. Gleig relates: '. . . after they had walked together for a while, in an autumnal evening on the beach beneath the castle, the Duke would stop short and say: "Now, Arbuthnot, you've been out long enough. The dew is falling, and you'll catch cold; you must go in."

Charles 'Gosh' Arbuthnot
(The Victoria and Albert Museum)

And like a child obeying the behest of its mother or its nurse, Arbuthnot, not always without a brief remonstrance, would leave the Duke to continue his walk alone, and withdraw into the Castle.'

Arbuthnot, in his turn, fussed over his friend. After supper the Duke would retire to the drawing room where it was his habit to fall asleep in his armchair while reading the newspaper by candlelight. Silently, he would retrieve the dropped paper and extinguish the flame. . .

But all this is to anticipate. There were still many happy hours left for the three companions to share together, especially in those early carefree years at Walmer Castle.

Mrs Arbuthnot's *Journal*, July 1829:

21st – We left London on the 17th of this month and came to Walmer Castle, where we mean to stay till the end of next week. The Duke got this house when he succeeded Lord Liverpool as Lord Warden, and he is very much delighted with it. It certainly is the most charming marine chateau that ever was, close upon the sea, the Downs constantly full of shipping coming in and going out, and a very comfortable house with a beautiful pleasure ground and quite sheltered by plantations. I dare say he will generally spend the summer here. We are quite alone with him; but the Esterhazys are coming the end of the week.

29th – We have been passing our time here very agreeably. I have bathed almost every day which has done me a great good, and the fresh air, tranquility and comfort have wrought a miracle upon the Duke; he has grown fat and looks better than I have seen him for years. . .

And in that same year Harriet Arbuthnot wrote to Lady Shelley:

You cannot think how well he is looking; he has neither pale cheek nor a long chin, but is fat and florid, and more like my picture than he has been for years. I really never saw him better, or in better spirits. I think it is Walmer that has done him so much good.

*

The Duke was a popular and generous host and according to one guest 'so full of fun and anecdote'. Yet he was soon regretting his famed hospitality. 'The whole of the world chooses to visit me, and at Walmer Castle,' he despaired, noting practically that: 'the accommodation of the house is not infinite.' The most popular guest was Wellington's niece, Priscilla, Lady Burghersh, who visited the castle with her young family every summer from 1831 to 1841. Her father, Lord Maryborough (William Wellesley-Pole, the Duke's elder brother, later the third Lord Mornington) became Captain of Deal Castle after Lord Carrington's death in 1838.

Other welcome guests were Lord and Lady Salisbury who had been constant companions at Walmer Castle from the beginning of the Duke's occupation. For these intimate acquaintances the Duke readily admitted that: 'This house stretches handsomely at times.'

Lord Ellesmere stayed for several days in November 1835 and found the distinguished company included Lord Mahon, Lord and Lady Salisbury, Lady Burghersh, Lord Rosslyn, Mr Arbuthnot and Lady Stanhope together with Mr Rogers, a forgotten local poet, and Mr Jones, junior, an optician from London. 'He was employed to put to rights a good-sized astronomic reflecting telescope, still at Walmer, and stayed a week amusing the Duke and Mr Arbuthnot with his scientific talk.'

To entertain his illustrious guests, the Duke often employed singers, one of whom was Miss Mary Ann Jervis, rather unflatteringly referred to in the Duke's letters as 'The Siren'. She arrived at Walmer with her father, Lord St Vincent, and having a fine voice 'sang from morning to night, and night to morning'. The Duke liked music, especially when sung by an attractive woman, and soon there was talk of romance between the old soldier and this eccentric female who was back singing at Walmer the following year. . .

Their 'romance' ended abruptly, however, for she flirted with the Duke so outrageously that she was eventually sent packing! It greatly amused the Duke to write to Lady Salisbury on 26 October 1836 that he was 'supposed to be going to marry her'. He sighed with relief when he learned of her marriage shortly afterwards to an Indian Nabob. In her place another celebrated singer, known puzzlingly as 'The Grisi', was employed to sing at castle gatherings in her place.

Often the Duke's hospitality was sorely tried. For instance, in October 1836, there were at Walmer: a painter (Lilley), a sculptor (Campbell Hall) and his assistant, all busily working creatively in the dining room. When they eventually left the Duke exclaimed with evident relief to Lady Salisbury: 'Thank God I have done with the artists.' Lilley, however, after eighteen sittings at Walmer Castle, went on to Stratfield Saye where he exacted nine more!

Wellington's favourite walk was on the castle ramparts,
also known as 'the platform'

But there were more serious invasions. In October, 1833, the Duke and Duchess of Cumberland and Prince George dined and slept at Walmer on their way to Dover; in October, 1837, Princess Augusta of Saxony, who was on holiday in England, attended a luncheon at the castle; and two years later the Duke and Duchess of Cambridge, with their daughter, Princess Augusta, stayed from 3rd until 8th October. 'It is a charming thing to be a Boniface,' declared the Duke when they were out with the harriers on 2nd October. 'To find room for them in that small castle . . . and the gentlemen's gentlemen and the ladies' ladies. It is as bad as quartering an army.'

Things were certainly done in style. During that month when the royal party stayed at Walmer Lord Mahon walked on the castle ramparts with the Duke and dined there afterwards in a party of eighteen. . . In the evening there was a concert, 'the Duke having engaged several vocalists from London and invited most of the neighbours. All went off extremely well and was over by half-past eleven.' Another dinner and concert followed two days later and the final function in honour of their Royal Highnesses, was attended by over one hundred guests from as far afield as Ramsgate and Dover.

*

Lord Mahon – later Earl Stanhope – was a close friend of the Duke. He was frequently in the area when visiting his mother, Countess Stanhope, who resided at The Lodge along Walmer Beach, and also his grandfather, Lord Carrington, Captain of Deal Castle. Often he was invited to dine at Walmer Castle and when there he secretly noted the intimate table-talk of his host which he published in 1888 as *Conversations with the Duke of Wellington: 1831 – 1851.*

Celebrities who visited the castle over these years included the Prince of Liechtenstein, Lord Bute, Lord Brougham, Lady Charlotte Greville, Lady Sandwich, Lord and Lady Hardwick . . . and many others. The centrepiece of the Duke's dining table whenever a distinguished company gathered was a silver épergne bearing a Latin inscription and surmounted by a figure representing Victory, presented by the officers after the battles of Roliça and Vimeiro. On such occasions the Duke talked informatively and freely and always Lord Mahon was an attentive listener. He noted the turn of the conversation from military matters and politics to an extraordinary range of topics: balloon ascents, martello towers, national education, penny postage, literature, spies, elephants, old age, medicine, memory, madness . . .

Lord Mahon accompanied the Duke on many local expeditions: following the harriers in the vicinity of Northbourne Mill; attending the christening of the Revd George Gleig's child at Ash; reviewing Lord Carrington's regiment at Canterbury and inspecting preparations for an experimental battery beyond Sandown Castle.

On one of his jaunts about the countryside in his phaeton, the Duke explored the ruins of Richborough Castle with Lady Wilton . . . and he pointed this out as the possible landing place of Julius Caesar. Here his history was truly at fault for the site was much closer to home. Indeed, Walmer Castle probably covers the exact spot!

*

The Countess Stanhope was the recipient of a greatly coveted artefact. When she expressed the need of good field glasses, the Duke sent over his own, complete with leather case and straps and a humorous note: 'You were talking of a glass, and I send you one of my field-glasses which used to be excellent. The fog is so thick that I cannot try to see you by the sight of it but I dare say it will show you all our doings here on the ramparts. . . You will think that I wish you to see everything through my eyes.'

The Duke of Wellington's telescopes now displayed at Stratfield Saye House (Photograph reproduced by kind permission of His Grace the Duke of Wellington, KG, Stratfield Saye House, Hampshire)

Later, it was revealed that this was the very telescope the Duke of Wellington had used at the Battle of Waterloo. Naturally, it was much prized in the family. When he realised how much pleasure his gift had afforded, the Duke presented Lord Mahon with a second telescope – this time it was the one he had employed on his Peninsular campaigns.

Eventually the Duke's kindness was repaid when Lady Mahon brought back from the Continent a small ivory figure of Napoleon nonchalantly seated and leaning against the back of a chair peering through binoculars. It was supposed to strike the same posture as when Napoleon commanded the Battle of Wagram. This figure the Duke awarded prime position on his mantlepiece though he insisted disparagingly that the Emperor was peering through opera glasses!

*

After Waterloo the Duke swore that he had fought his last battle and retreated into politics. He was appointed Prime Minister for the Tory party in January 1828 when his inability to adjust to the times led to battles of a different sort. His obstinate opposition to the Reform Bill, which provided for the fairer redistribution of Parliamentary seats, introduced in March 1831, resulted in his great unpopularity. Angry mobs stormed Apsley House (where the body of Kitty Pakenham, the first Duchess of Wellington, lay awaiting burial) and they even set fire to his church pew at Stratfield Saye.

His unpopularity followed him to Walmer. Gleig relates how one evening, after dusk, a mysterious stranger, wrapped in a seaman's greatcloak, was ushered into his vicarage study with details of a plot to kill the Duke. The intruder, named Underwood, had been a spy during the Napoleonic Wars while carrying on a lucrative smuggling trade with the Continent. He had overheard a plan hatched in a local public house to attack the Duke's carriage on a lonely stretch of road between Sandwich and the turnpike at Deal.

News was relayed to the Duke in London but he was determined to travel to Walmer that season. Duty called. Declaring bluntly that it was the responsibility of the local magistrates to protect all His Majesty's subjects, 'particularly those acting under the King's authority', he set off for Deal – though at an earlier hour than intended.

Several gentlemen of the county armed themselves and met the Duke's carriage between Wingham and Ash and escorted his conveyance to the drawbridge at Walmer. Once the carriage had safely turned in at the castle gate, the voluntary escort dispersed without attracting attention. Yet the Duke had not simply trusted himself to the protection of his friends: he had stuffed a brace of double-barrelled pistols into the pocket of his britzka.

No enemy appeared. Rumours died hard and there were still fears for the Duke's safety during this critical period of his political career. He wrote to assure Harriet Arbuthnot:

Walmer Castle
10 November 1831

I passed yesterday at Dover. I was again threatened with sudden Death! I was told that the Mayor had sworn in 200 Special Constables. I drove into

35

town alone, was received with great Respect by everybody, walked all over Town after the business of the Harbour Sessions was finished, and I don't think I met a respectable Man who did not pull off His Hat; and I don't hear a Word of Reform or a whisper of discontent or disrespect.

With all these reports and alarms of attempts on his life how was it that the Duke felt able to stroll about the district apparently unprotected? Only after his death was this secret revealed:

An officer in the Regiment quartered in the neighbourhood walked to Walmer Castle soon after the Duke's death. He asked his servant whether he could spare any article, however insignificant, of the Duke. The servant said, 'There are a lot of umbrellas in that corner, if you like, you can have one of them.' The officer took up one of the umbrellas, and endeavoured to open it. To his surprise he drew out a sword. He pointed this out. The servant replied, 'Oh, yes; there is a sword in every umbrella.' This, no doubt, would have given the Duke a chance, who walked about London, and elsewhere, absolutely unattended, had he been attacked. (Sir William Fraser, *Words On Wellington.*)

*

In the autumn of 1832, the 60th Foot was stationed at Dover. The Duke was in residence and, as was his custom, all the officers rode over to Walmer to pay their respects and leave their calling cards. Lord Douro, Wellington's eldest son, was also stationed at Dover at the time but neglected to join their company. He experienced his father's stern discipline. Raikes has the story:

Shortly after came an invitation from his Grace to dinner, including all the officers, excepting Lord Douro. The Major who received the note, quite confused, knew not how to act and shewed it to Lord Douro, who was equally puzzled, tho' he knew it must have some meaning. To solve the difficulty he went forthwith to see the Duke at Walmer who with great good humour told him: 'I make no distinctions in the service; those gentlemen who paid me the compliment of a visit I invited to dinner; you were not of the number and so I omitted you.'

Curzon adds the comment: 'In short, he was a martinet, having in him that element of the regimental sergeant-major which is always found in the best British regimental officers; and he carried into the nineteenth century a formality which belonged rather to the eighteenth.'

The Duke held dinner parties two or three times a week during his autumnal residences and his invitation always extended to the officers quartered at Dover

Castle. Captain Watts, the last Captain of Walmer Castle, discovered that on one such occasion a young officer had accidentally been passed over and, realising how disappointed the youth would be, he mentioned the oversight to the Duke. 'How many are there to dinner?' the Duke enquired; and when informed that the table would hold an additional guest he added: 'By all means, write and invite him too.'

*

In the autumn of 1835, Princess Victoria was staying with her mother, the Duchess of Kent, at Ramsgate. In October, they were joined by the King and Queen of Belgium and the royal party was invited over as guests of the Duke at Walmer Castle.

The wooden bridge over the moat leads to the celebrated gardens

Wellington's niece, Lady Burghersh, helped him to do the honours. Later she wrote an account of the royal visit to her husband:

Everything went off very well indeed to-day. The day was beautiful. The King and Queen of the Belgians arrived exactly at two o'clock in the same carriage with the Duchess of Kent and Princess Victoria. The Duke of Wellington and I went to meet them on the drawbridge, and brought them up the outside of the staircase to the ramparts (where nearly all the company were assembled) the lower battery firing a salute.

The Broad Walk at Walmer Castle

The scene was beautiful; the whole of the beach in front of the castle and the roads leading to Deal and to the village were filled with people; colours being hoisted at the different places along the coast and on the ships, of which, fortunately, there were quantities in the Downs. The only drawback was that we were disappointed of getting a band from Canterbury; so there was no music.

After walking about the ramparts and speaking to the company the King and Queen went with the Duke round the garden, but the Princess Victoria had a little cold; I stayed in the drawing-room with her and the Duchess of Kent. . . As the crowds outside were eager to see Princess Victoria, I asked the Duchess of Kent if she might come out for a moment to shew herself, and I fetched my ermine tippet for her, which she put on, and came out on the ramparts and was much cheered. Luncheon was very handsome and laid for 40 people in the two rooms.

When they went away the Duke and I went down to the entrance again and put them in the carriage and the mob cheered very much, and as they drove off they gave one more cheer for the Duke.

Less than two years later Victoria succeeded to the throne. Her Majesty recalled her happy visit to Walmer and in the third year of her marriage to Prince Albert she spent a month's informal holiday with her young family at the castle.

*

A high point of Wellington's life at Walmer Castle! But there were sad moments too. After Harriet Arbuthnot's death the Duke had found a new confidante in the gay and charming society hostess, Fanny, Lady Salisbury. She was his lively companion at all of his homes and often brought her young family down to stay for months at a time at Walmer. She was also the recipient of hundreds of letters from her 'beau'.

When she, too, died at an early age the Duke was inconsolable. Lady Salisbury had succumbed to dropsy in the summer and expired in the autumn of 1837. Immediately Wellington received the sad news he went into mourning and sealed his letters with black wax. Three weeks later he was found speechless and temporarily blind on the floor of his study at Walmer Castle.

*

An infant school was started in 1838 through the endeavours of Miss S. E. French, who leased for this purpose a coachhouse and stable, together with a yard for a playground, situated in Cambridge Road, Lower Walmer. Two rooms were added for the mistress, at a cost, including further alterations, of £104. 10s. Yearly rent of these premises amounted to £5. The Duke was named among the subscribers. (He was also named among the subscribers to the building of Saint Saviour's Church, a chapel-of-ease to Old Saint Mary's, erected for the boatmen along the Strand, opened in 1849.)

The Duke's affection for children was renowned. Among his favourite visitors were his grandchildren. He simply doted on them. If they were ill, he was a devoted nurse. When they were in high spirits he could perfectly match their mood for he might be seen playing football on the castle ramparts or throwing cushions across the drawing room in an energetic mock Battle of Waterloo.

Once, Lord William de Ros was returning from a visit to Walmer with his wife and daughter, Blanche, on a steamer from Deal to London when an irate

St Saviour's, the boatmen's church, along Walmer Strand. The Duke headed the subscription list for its building. The steeple was later struck by lightning

passenger accosted him and complained: 'I really think you ought to warn your little girl not to romance as she does. She has just told me this morning that she had a pillow fight with the Duke of Wellington.' Embarrassed, Lord de Ros had to admit that what his daughter had said was true!

In 1837, the ailing Lord Robert Grosvenor took his wife abroad for a holiday and left his children for several months in the care of the Duke. Two years later, the children came again to stay at Walmer Castle where there seemed to be a whole swarm of youngsters about the place. One morning the Duke invited his young friends to breakfast at which there was a large assembly of distinguished guests. Sir Algernon West, whose father had built himself a house on the beach at Walmer, recalled:

He had just returned from Windsor, where at whist he had won a few shillings, the first that had been coined in the Queen's reign. My sister says: 'We were playing on the ramparts, and he came up to us and he said to me, "Would you like a picture of the Queen?" and putting his hand in his pocket he brought out three or four of these bright new shillings and gave me one; seeing my sister looking on very wistfully he added, "And would you like one too?" I think he gave one also to Miss de Ros and Miss Hardinge.'

One morning the children of Lord and Lady Grosvenor showed disappointment that the postbag contained an enormous amount of correspondence for the Duke but no letters for themselves. Next day they received a large assortment of mail containing good advice for the day written in the Duke's own hand. After the introduction of the penny post in 1840 his own grandchildren used to gather round him before breakfast to collect the envelopes from his letters so that they could pick off the seals and collect the stamps.

The Duke's favourite corner in his study gave a view southwards over the English Channel

Lord Grosvenor's son, later Lord Ebury, related the strangest story about the Iron Duke: 'All that I remember is . . . that on one occasion the Duke appeared in our quarters, as it might be a Christmas tree, with quite a number of toys attached to his person, of which he disburdened himself for our benefit.' Sadly, this episode ended in tears for one of the party, Blanche de Ros, in her excitement, slipped on the ramparts and cracked her skull.

A charming engraving highlighting the country aspect of the castle in Victorian times

The wooded grounds of Walmer Castle provided an enticing adventure playground for these young visitors. Julian Fane, one of the sons of the Duke's niece, Priscilla, Lady Burghersh (later Countess of Westmorland) was once caught raiding the fruit trees by the gardener and duly admonished. 'Never mind, let's go to the Duke,' the lad boldly suggested to his companions, 'he always allows everything and gives you what you like.'

His sister, Rose, later recalled: 'I am sometimes inclined to laugh when I read descriptions of his sternness, at our childish impressions of his house as a Liberty Hall where we could do as we pleased, in contradistinction to my grandfather's who was a great martinet, and whom we were afraid of but we never thought of being the least afraid of the Duke.' It was to no avail that Lady Burghersh complained that the Duke spoiled her children so outrageously.

Then there is the amusing story of the Java sparrows which the Burghersh children had smuggled into Deal Castle, at that time occupied by their grandfather, Lord Maryborough. Lord Maryborough was by no means so indulgent towards children as his brother, the Duke, and had given firm orders that pets were not to be kept in the castle. Unfortunately, the twittering of the birds disclosed their presence and they were immediately banished. The children walked over to Walmer to present their problem to the Duke who agreed to keep the birds himself until he returned to town.

But the Duke's kindness towards children extended further than his own family. Pritchard, the Deal historian, states that the Duke always carried with him a supply of sovereigns and half sovereigns through each of which was drilled a small hole for a ribbon, either blue or red. Whenever he came across a group of children he would ask them: 'Are you for the army or the navy?' According to how they answered he would hang about their neck the appropriate medallion – blue for the navy; red for the army. Only once did he make a blunder. He rashly promised one lucky child a commission in the Guards – 'But I'm a dirl, Mr Dook.'

On one occasion the Duke's youthful companion romping in the grounds was Robert Cecil, who later thrice became Queen Victoria's Prime Minister and subsequently Lord Warden.

There was a strict order against strangers wandering from the road leading to the gate and straying into the gardens or shrubberies surrounding Walmer Castle. It happened, on one occasion, that a lady, ignorant of this rule, strolled into the paddock with her two children and she received a stern rebuke from one of the servants. At that precise moment the Duke rode by and asked what was the matter. Nervously, the lady offered her apology.

'Oh, never mind, never mind,' interrupted the Duke. 'You're quite welcome to go where you will.' Then, as he was about to ride away, he turned and said, 'By the way, bring the children here tomorrow at one o'clock and I'll show them all about the place myself.'

As desired, the lady returned to the castle on the following day and was surprised to find the Duke had prepared a hearty meal for her and the children. After a conducted tour over the castle and gardens, the Duke presented each of the youngsters with the inevitable half-sovereign suspended from a blue ribbon before sending them on their way.

*

One of the principal delights of Walmer Castle is the gardens. During the Duke's residence there existed an expanse of 'very pretty pleasure ground and walks among trees and shrubs' landwards of the castle while the circular moat served as a vegetable plot. Undeniably, the Duke appreciated the natural beauty of the grounds – a handsome lime was pointed out as a favourite tree under which the Duke sat and read – but he seemed indifferent towards their upkeep. He took no pleasure in strolling through them although he willingly lent out his garden key. When his friend, Miss Angela Burdett-Coutts, wrote asking for some cuttings from Walmer Castle that she might plant in her own garden at Holly Lodge, the Duke responded that, although he was 'flattered' by her request, he regarded the project as time-wasting.

The Duke's gardener at Walmer, far from being a professional, was an ex-guardsman who became a warder when Wellington was Constable of the Tower of London. Mr Townsend, as a sergeant in the Grenadiers, distinguished himself in the crowning charge of Waterloo: his halberd was shot from him and a cannon ball carried off his shako.

Sergeant Townsend was appointed to the post of head gardener under the most peculiar circumstances. Shortly after Wellington became Lord Warden he received a letter from Sergeant Townsend complaining that he had been discharged from service without a pension. Promptly, the Duke replied: 'Field-Marshal the Duke of Wellington would be happy to see Sergeant Townsend at Apsley House on Friday at noon.'

Punctually, at the appointed time, Sergeant Townsend made his appearance and he had scarcely been seated in the ante-room when the Duke arrived. During the interview His Grace enquired, 'Do you know anything about gardening?' and upon receiving a negative reply, added, 'Then learn, learn, and come here this day fortnight at the same hour.'

Pending the interview, Sergeant Townsend endeavoured to learn at least something about gardening but naturally he found the art difficult to master in so short a space of time. Obedient to orders he presented himself a second time at Apsley House. This time the Duke began with, 'Take the place of gardener at Walmer Castle, twenty-eight shillings a week, a house, and all that.' 'But I know nothing about gardening,' protested the Sergeant. 'Nor do I, nor do I,' said the Duke bluntly. 'Take your place at once.'

Upon his arrival at Walmer, Sergeant Townsend found that instructions had preceded him for he was comfortably lodged in a cottage, fully furnished and equipped with everything that would ensure his ease. For several weeks he employed someone to teach him the difference between flowers and weeds! Hearing that the Duke was about to visit the castle, Townsend prepared a speech in his mind in order to thank His Grace properly for his kindness but he never found the opportunity.

On one occasion he resolved to get up very early and present himself purposely at the precise spot where the Duke was accustomed to take his early morning exercise. Touching his hat, he was about to speak when the Duke cut him short with, 'How d'ye do?' and passed on. Sergeant Townsend never did find the opportunity to express gratitude to his noble, and generous, patron.

Visitors to Walmer Castle were welcomed in the Duke's absence and shown round the castle and its gardens by Mrs Allen, the Duke's housekeeper. One visitor expressed surprise at the number of robins darting among the hawthorn bushes and was informed that, as the Duke evinced a great fondness for these plucky birds, every effort was made by the staff to encourage them to breed in the grounds.

Starlings once saved the Duke from an embarrassing situation. Curzon relates mischievously how the Duke, by an accident to the bolt, was locked in the lavatory! This exceptionally small room had one tiny horizontal window through which it was just possible to peer through the thick castle walls. The Duke was reluctant to raise the alarm by shouting as he knew how quickly tales would spread about the neighbourhood concerning his mental state. Opposite the window was a tower covered with ivy in which the Duke had noticed starlings nesting. Accordingly, he waited patiently and when all the birds flew

This coastal path became one of the Duke's favourite strolls
(The Victoria and Albert Museum)

out he deduced that someone was passing. Only then did he call out to be rescued!

The Duke's favourite exercise was to stroll about the castle ramparts particularly in the early morning when they caught the eastern sun. An alternative walk was along the path at the top of the beach directly in front of the castle which was originally laid out by William Pitt for use by The Preventive Men who preceded the Coast Guard. There he was a familiar figure in his blue jacket, white duck trousers and, on breezy days, a top hat.

The green in front of Walmer Castle, where a sloop or brig-of-war was permanently stationed offshore in wartime, remained the property of the Lord Warden. The actual boundary on either side, however, was supposed to be ninety feet. Earl Granville placed stones to mark his territory on the beach – at the same time as planting clumps of trees and bushes as a windbreak – though his claim on this scrubland was somewhat generous.

There are indications, too, from descriptions and engravings that Walmer Castle was nearer to the sea than it is today. 'After coming through the village of Walmer, you see the entrance of the Castle away to the right. It is situated pretty nearly on the water's edge, and at the bottom of a little dell, about a furlong or so from the turnpike road. . .' (William Cobbett's *Rural Rides*.)

Traditionally, distinguished residents of the castle have been invited to plant a tree or a shrub in the grounds to mark the period of their occupancy. Elvin, the Walmer historian, supplies a list: an acacia planted by Queen Elizabeth I, a palm by Lord Clive, a tulip tree by Pitt and a lime by Fox. The Duke of Wellington was prevailed upon to plant something and he chose a sprig from the willow that grew over Napoleon's tomb at St Helena. Apparently, this tree survived until Earl Granville's time when a cutting was transplanted in the moat.

The tradition of distinguished visitors planting a tree at Walmer continues to this day. H.M. the Queen Mother, who is the present Lord Warden, planted a Turkey Oak which continues to thrive despite recent hurricanes.

There is a persistent local legend that the clumps of ilexes growing in the paddock on the north side of the castle were planted to illustrate the position of British squares of infantry at the height of the Battle of Waterloo. The story has good provenance (Sir Gerald Wollaston) but the trees were planted after Wellington's demise and the notion that the Duke gave precise instructions for their site would seem to be pure fantasy.

The path directly in front of the castle was originally laid by Pitt for the use of the Preventive Men

Chapter Three

A PORTRAIT OF THE IRON DUKE

DURING HIS military life, the Duke of Wellington, as supreme commander, expected to make his own decisions and act without consultation. His political career, which lasted for more than thirty-five years, was often conducted in the same manner but with a party to lead and a country to govern, the result was often disastrous.

The Duke's popularity was greatly assured, however, in the summer of 1839 for it marked the first decade of his term as Lord Warden. His installation had taken place almost entirely without ceremony but now the time had come to celebrate. A banquet was planned whose magnificence was marked by almost unprecedented splendour.

Mr Edmunds, a local architect, was challenged to design a temporary building as a grand venue for the festivities in Dover. Twenty thousand sightseers were expected to witness this historic event and shopkeepers were not slow to produce souvenirs. A superbly detailed medal – showing the Duke's head in profile on the obverse with Dover Castle on the reverse – was struck to mark the occasion.

A huge square pavilion was erected on land formerly owned by the Priory opposite the Maison Dieu. The project took almost five months to complete by one hundred workmen at a cost of £1,200. This curious temporary building covered an area of 20,240 square feet and involved 20,000 cubic feet of timber. Wisely, particular attention was paid to waterproofing the roof and this considerable problem was solved by the substitution of tarred cartridge paper for sailcloth. The square ground plan of this temporary structure which was in itself enormous (forty feet square) was later presented to the Duke. It is now lost.

Portrait medal struck to commemorate The Duke of Wellington's first decade as Lord Warden (Dover Museum)

47

The Cinque Ports Dinner (Dover Museum)

William Burgess (1805–61), the celebrated artist from Dover, was commissioned to prepare two drawings to commemorate the event – to which he added a third print of the later Cinque Ports Ball. His impressive engravings record the event in fine detail although he may have employed some licence in respect of the size of the building.

The huge pavilion near the Maison Dieu in Dover where the celebrations were held in honour of the Duke during the summer of 1839 (Dover Museum)

The imaginative decoration of the 'Wellington Pavilion' was kept a closely guarded secret right up until the day of the banquet. At the far end was a dais on which sat the Duke of Wellington and seventy eminent guests. Above, the royal coat-of-arms surrounded by flags of the Cinque Ports Volunteers and the Duke's coat-of-arms appeared alongside a trophy in the form of a cuirass, a helmet and other arms taken from the field of Waterloo. This striking display was hung against a suspended backcloth of soft pink and white stripes. More armaments and suits of armour decorated the building borrowed from the Tower of London and Dover Castle. Tapestries, paintings and furniture were also lent by private persons for the occasion. The interior was illuminated by eleven floral gas-lit chandeliers wrought by a London craftsman. Yet the most spectacular aspect of these lavish decorations, however, were the transparencies on the rooflights exquisitely painted by Burgess.

On Friday 30 August 1839, the day of the banquet, six steamboats arrived from Ramsgate and Margate conveying two thousand passengers to watch the

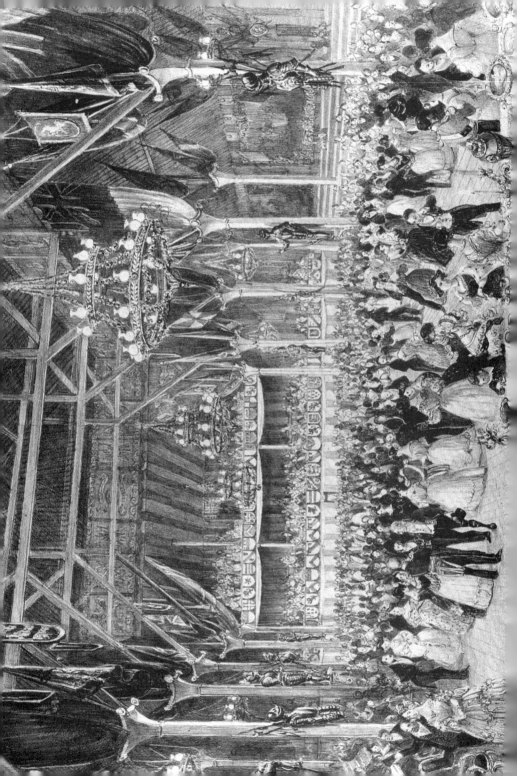

festivities. Yet another steamer from Rye brought further spectators. These crowds were entertained by band concerts on the pier and firework displays on Dover Seafront.

As the hour for dinner approached, the streets and avenues leading to Priory Meadow were crowded with finely dressed ladies and gentlemen. Shortly before the arrival of the Duke, a guard of honour of the 27th Regiment, under the command of Captain Smith (who had been severely wounded at Waterloo) marched from Dover Castle to Maison Dieu. A few minutes before five o'clock, the Duke, dressed in his Lord Warden's uniform, was observed approaching from Walmer in his phaeton and pair. He drove proudly through the streets and was greeted at every turn by hearty cheers from thousands of inhabitants and visitors. Graciously, he acknowledged their greetings and alighted at Maison Dieu.

A salute from the guns of the artillery on Dover Heights gave intimation of the arrival of the illustrious guest while the bells from numerous churches struck up a mighty tintinnabulation.

Inside the Wellington Pavilion over 1,500 gentlemen sat down to dine. They dined off exquisite plates and used gold-handled cutlery. For this privilege they had been charged £1. 11s. 6d (one and a half guineas) per head. Although there were sufficient waiters several guests complained about the inefficient service.

The menu was tantalising:

29 quarters of lamb	56 dishes of roast veal
56 dishes of boiled beef	28 dishes of roast beef
120 couple of chickens	40 turkey poults
28 hams	56 tongues
20 pigeon pies	240 venison pies
200 lobsters	200 salads
180 fruit pies	160 custard puddings
plus1 bottle of wine per guest	

In addition the Duke's table was served with soups and joints of venison.

This sumptuous repast was watched from a special 'gallery of beauty' by 500 ladies who were treated to jelly and ice cream. The proceedings were marred only by unpleasant wrangling regarding who should propose the health of the Lord Warden: Lord Guilford *versus* Lord Brougham. Lord Brougham won in the end and as a consequence the more appropriate local speaker declined even to attend. Lord Brougham's fawning speech, in which he compared Wellington to Caesar, Hannibal, Marlborough and Napoleon, was judged by Greville to be 'tawdry' since the Duke 'hates to be praised'. On the contrary the Duke succumbed to this flattery, for he deemed the speech 'admirable'.

Opposite — The Cinque Ports Ball (Dover Museum)

*

The Cinque Ports Ball – a famous occasion – took place a short while later on 5 September 1839. Almost one thousand guests attended. 'Mount's Band' was engaged (Rye Amateur Band offered to perform but was politely declined) and positioned on the dais. On the gallery at the eastern end of the Wellington Pavilion the bands of the 27th and 90th Regiments 'played alternately delightful airs between the dances'. The Duke, who was fond of dancing, arrived with his party at 9 p.m. and stayed until almost midnight. The evening was judged to be a tremendous success for it was noted that, despite the withdrawal of several more grand parties, the festivities continued until the early hours of the following morning.

The Cinque Ports celebrations had confirmed the public's high regard and admiration for their Lord Warden. The Duke of Wellington – through hard industry and endeavour coupled with active concern for the welfare of his neighbours in all walks of life – was once more at the height of popularity.

*

The Duke was constantly besieged by artists and sculptors who desired to capture his likeness. In December, 1838, the City of Liverpool commissioned Benjamin Haydon to paint the Duke's portrait. It was intended as a fanciful composition entitled 'Wellington musing on the Field of Waterloo' – twenty-three years after the battle. More, it was to be entirely innovative with the Duke standing with his back to the viewer – a daring pose which eventually won the artist a huge wager! Haydon wrote requesting a sitting and, although the reply was in the affirmative, the Duke was reluctant to name a precise date.

Meanwhile Haydon worked busily preparing the canvas. Early in the new year the design was rubbed in; he borrowed a sketch of the Duke's horse, 'Copenhagen', to copy; then toured the battlefield. He even traced the Duke's saddler, Whippey, who readily agreed to equip a horse with identical trappings to those worn on the day of victory. A request to borrow the Duke's clothing, however, was met with a blunt refusal: 'The Duke hopes that he will have a cessation of note-writing about pictures,' since 'he must decline to lend anybody his clothes, arms or equipment.'

Undaunted, the indomitable artist tracked down the Duke's tailor and ordered himself a pair of trousers in identical pattern . . . 'so that I shall kill two birds with one stone – wear 'em and paint 'em'.

Undeniably, the Duke of Wellington had not so far been encouraging.

*

Eventually, this missive arrived:

Walmer Castle
October 9th, 1839

The Duke of Wellington presents his compliments to Mr. Haydon. If Mr. Haydon will be so kind as to come to Walmer Castle, whenever it may suit him, the Duke will have it in his power to sit to him for a picture for certain gentlemen at Liverpool.

*

Overjoyed, Benjamin Haydon hastily packed his bags and made for Walmer Castle still uncertain of the reception he was to receive. At the Duke's warm hospitality, he could not have been more surprised. He wrote a very full account of his expedition in his journal:

OCTOBER 11th – Left town by steamer for Ramsgate. Got in at half past six, dined and set off in a chaise for Walmer, where I arrived safely in hard rain. A great bell was rung on my arrival; and after taking tea and dressing, I was ushered into the drawing-room, where sat His Grace with Sir Astley Cooper, Mr Arbuthnot, and Mr Booth, who had served with His Grace in Spain. His Grace welcomed me heartily, asked how I came down, and fell again into general conversation. . .
    I studied his fine head intensely – Arbuthnot had begun to doze.
    I was like a lamp new trimmed, and could have listened all night. The Duke gave a tremendous yawn, and said, 'It is time to go to bed.' Candles

A view of Walmer Castle with the port of Deal in the distance

were rung for. He took two, and lighted them himself. The rest lighted their own. The Duke took one and gave me (being the stranger) the other, and led the way. At an old view of Dover, in the hall, he stopped and explained about the encroachment of the sea. I studied him again – we all held up our candles. Sir Ashley went to Mr Pitt's bed-room and said, 'God bless Your Grace.' They dropped off – His Grace and I, and the valet going on. I came to my room, and said, 'God bless Your Grace.' I saw him going into his. When I got to bed I could not sleep. Good God, I thought, here am I tête-a-tête with the greatest man on earth, and the noblest – the conqueror of Napoleon – sitting with him, talking to him, sleeping near him. His mind is unimpaired; his conversation powerful, humorous, witty, argumentative, sound, moral. . .

SATURDAY – At ten o'clock was breakfasted – The Duke, Sir Astley, Mr Booth and myself. He put me on his right. 'Which will ye have, black tea or green?' 'Black, Your Grace.' 'Bring black.' Black was brought, and I ate a hearty breakfast. In the midst six dear healthy, noisy children were brought to the windows. 'Let them in,' said the Duke, and in they came, and rushed over to him, saying, 'How d'ye do, Duke? How d'ye do, Duke?' One boy, young Grey, roared, 'I want some tea, Duke.' 'You shall have it, if you promise not to slop it over me, as you did yesterday.' Toast and tea were then in demand. Three got on one side, and three on the other, and he hugged 'em all.

Tea was poured out and I saw little Grey try to slop it over the Duke's frock coat. Sir Astley said, 'You did not expect to see this.' They all then rushed out on the leads, by the cannon, and after breakfast I saw the Duke romping with the whole of them, and one of them gave His Grace a devil of a thump. I went round to my bed-room. The children came to the window, and a dear little black-eyed girl began romping. I put my head out and said, 'I'll catch you.' Just as I did this, the Duke, who did not see me, put his head out at the door close to my room, No. 10, which leads to the leads, and said, 'I'll catch ye! Ha, ha, I've got ye!' at which they all ran away. He looked at them, laughed and went in.

He then told me to choose my room and get my light in order, and after hunting he would sit. I did so, and about two he gave me an hour. I hit his grand, upright, manly expression. He looked like an eagle who had put on human shape, and had got silvery with age and service. At first I was a little affected, but I hit his features and all went off. Riding hard had made him rosy and dozy. His colour was fresh. All the portraits are too pale. I found that to imagine he could not go through any duty raised the lion. 'Does the light hurt your Grace's eyes?' 'Not at all,' and he stared at the light as much as to say, 'I'll see if you shall make me give in, Signor Light.'

Sketch of the Iron Duke made by Benjamin Haydon at Walmer in 1839 in preparation for his painting, 'The Duke of Wellington musing on the field of Waterloo' (reproduced by kind permission of His Grace the Duke of Wellington, KG, Stratfield Saye House, Hampshire)

'Twas a noble head. I saw nothing of that peculiar expression of mouth the sculptors gave him, bordering on simpering. His colour was beautiful and fleshy, his lips compressed and energetic. I foolishly said, 'Don't let me fatigue Your Grace.' 'Well, sir,' he said, 'I'll give you an hour and a half. Tomorrow is Sunday. Monday I'll sit again.' I was delighted to see him pay his duty to Sunday. Up he rose. I opened the door, and hold this as the highest distinction of my life. He bowed and said, 'We dine at seven.'

At seven we dined. His Grace took half a glass of sherry and put water in it. I drank three glasses. Mr Arbuthnot one. We then went to the drawing-room where, putting a candle on each side of him, he read *The Standard* whilst I talked to Mr Arbuthnot. . .

I did not stay up to-night. I was tired, went to bed, and slept heartily. It was most interesting to see him reading away. I believe he read every iota. . . . I asked the Duke if Caesar did not land hereabouts. He said he believed near Richborough Castle.

SUNDAY – I found The Duke on the leads. After breakfast Mr Arbuthnot told me to go to the village church and ask for the Duke's pew. I walked, and was shown into a large pew near the pulpit. A few moments after the service had begun, the Duke and Mr Arbuthnot came up – no pomp, no servants in livery with a pile of books. The Duke came into the presence of His Maker without affectation, a simple human being. From the bare wainscot, the absence of curtains, the dirty green footstools, and common chairs, I feared I was in the wrong pew, and very quietly sat myself down in the Duke's place. Mr Arbuthnot squeezed my arm before it was too late and I crossed in an instant. The Duke pulled out his prayer-book, and followed the clergyman in the simplest way. I got deeply affected. Here was the greatest hero in the world, who had conquered the greatest genius, prostrating his heart and being before God in his venerable age, and praying for his mercy. However high his destiny above my own, here we were at least equal before our Creator. Here we were stripped of extrinsic distinctions; and I looked at this wonderful man with an interest and feeling that touched my imagination beyond belief, bowing his silvery hairs like the humblest labourer. Arthur Wellesley in the village church at Walmer. . .

The Duke after dinner retired and we all followed him. He then took *The Spectator*, and placing a candle on each side of his venerable head, read it through. . . After reading till his eyes were tired, he put down the paper. . . He then yawned, as he always did before retiring, and said, 'I'll give you an early sitting tomorrow at nine.' I wished His Grace a good night, and went to bed.

MONDAY – At half-past five I was up, set my palette, got all ready and went to work to get the head in from the drawing. By nine the door opened, and in he walked, looking extremely worn – his skin drawn right over his face; his eye was watery and aged; his head nodded a little. I put the chair; he mumbled, 'I'd as soon stand.' I thought, 'You will get tired,' but said nothing; down he sat – how altered from the fresh old man after Saturday's hunting! It affected me. He looked like an aged eagle beginning to totter from his perch. He took out his watch three times, and at ten up he got, and said, 'It's ten.' I opened the door and he went out. He had been impatient all the time.

At breakfast he brightened at the sight of the children, and after distributing toast and tea to them, I got him on art. . . He suddenly looked up at me and said, 'D'ye want another sitting?' I replied, 'If you please, Your Grace.' 'Very well; after hunting, I'll come.'

At three he came in to sit. . . Lady Burghersh came in also, and again he was fresher, but the feebleness of the morning still affected my heart. It is evident, at times, he is beginning to sink, though the sea air at Walmer keeps him up, and he is better than he was.

Lady Burghersh kept him talking; but the expression I had already hit was much finer than the present, and I resolved not to endanger what I had secured. I therefore corrected the figure and shoulders, and told Lady Burghersh I had done. 'He has done,' she said, 'and it's very fine.' 'Is it though?' said the Duke, 'I'm very glad.' 'And now,' said she, 'you must stand.' So up he got, and I sketched two views of his back, his hands, his legs, etc. I did him so instantaneously that his eagle eyes looked me right through several times, when he thought I was not looking. As it was a point of honour with him not to see any sketch connected with my picture, he never glanced that way. He looked at the designs for the House of Lords on the chimney-piece, but said nothing. He then retired, and appeared gay and better. He had put on a fine dashing waistcoat for the Russian Ambassador. At night, as I took leave of the Duke, he said, 'I hope you are satisfied. Goodbye.' I heard him go to bed after me, laughing, and he roared out to Arbuthnot, 'Goodnight.' I then heard him slam the door of his room, No. 11, next to mine, No. 10, but on the opposite side, and a little further on. I soon fell asleep; was off at six for Ramsgate, and dined at home at five.

My impression is that the Duke has begun to sink, though he will hold out for many years. His memory was healthy; his intellect unimpaired; but his physical vigour, I fear, is breaking now and then.

DECEMBER 23rd – Wrote the Duke (who has had a severe attack) a frank letter expressing my joy at his recovery, and sorrow at his illness, but telling His Grace he went too long without his food. I said I observed it at Walmer, and that from ten to half-past seven was too long without intervening sustenance.

Mr William Hulke, the general practitioner who attended the Duke
'Comarques' the Georgian residence of Mr Hulke still graces Deal's High

Wellington's Spartan existence was renowned and in later years he suffered several epileptic fits as a result of lack of meals or extreme cold. He had a strange philosophy regarding food: 'The great art of all is not to give the stomach too much to do.' Yet Lord Dalhousie, a later Lord Warden, rather pricked the bubble regarding the Duke's stoicism when he wrote to a colleague at Government House (10 July 1852) :

You mention having seen the Duke slipping along in a bleak east wind with white duck trousers on. Perhaps you are aware that there is not a little humbug in that affectation of hardiness by His Grace. He wears the white trousers, but there is always more than one pair of flannel drawers under them. . .

The Duke occasionally called upon the services of Mr William Hulke, described variously as 'apothecary', 'surgeon' and 'general family practitioner', who lived in Lower Street (now High Street), Deal. Once, while making a late night call to a patient in the vicinity of Walmer Castle, Mr Hulke disturbed a gang of smugglers unloading contraband on to the beach. Three pistols were fired in rapid succession and one bullet whistled past his head.

William Hulke, whose family was of Dutch descent, resided at 'Comarques', the red-bricked, double-fronted, Georgian mansion at the north end of the High Street. This imposing building incorporated a tunnel under the road for the ladies of the house to visit their father, William Hulke senior, who lived opposite. During World War Two a shell blasted the southern half of 'Comarques' which has since been meticulously restored and here the town's first telephone was installed (Tel: Deal 1).

When the Duke applied for medicines ('The Duke of Wellington requests that Mr Hulke will send him two pills each containing three grams of juniper powder') he sometimes enclosed an invitation to dinner ('The favour of an answer is desired.') At one such dinner party a partridge bone lodged in the Duke's throat and Mr Hulke was required to force it downwards thus saving him from choking. Mr Hulke's services were highly regarded by the Duke's family and he received an invitation to attend Wellington's funeral (riding in Carriage 14 which preceded the funeral car).

In 1839, the Duke had become extremely ill. That autumn he had stayed longer than usual at Walmer. On the afternoon of 19th November – a few days after Haydon left – he suffered a seizure. That morning he had gone out riding with a fur collar pulled tightly about his neck and an umbrella to ward off the constant drizzle. He seemed in fine spirits, though Lord Mahon noted that he 'seemed unwilling or unable to ride fast, often checking his horse with a jerk when it attempted to bound on.'

The Duke of Wellington relaxing in his study

Returning to the castle the Duke entered his bedroom to write several letters, then went into the drawing room to read the newspapers. Here he first noticed something was amiss for despite all his efforts he could not hold the paper still: it kept slipping from his fingers. Next he tried to 'walk it off' – a favourite remedy of his for threatened ailments – but this achieved nothing. Reluctantly, he retired to his bedroom, rang his bell and gave orders to send for Mr Hulke.

Before the order could be obeyed, however, the Duke's bell rang again and Kendall, his manservant, was horrified to find his master 'with his lower jaw dropped and moving so that notwithstanding his efforts to speak he could not explain what he wanted.' Failing to make himself understood, the Duke signalled Kendall to leave the room. Thoroughly alarmed, the faithful servant remained in the passage behind the door. When he heard a dull thud he ran in to find the Duke collapsed on the floor.

Kendall lifted his unconscious master on to his bed and sent William, the Duke's own footman, to fetch Lord Mahon. Immediately, the local doctors, Hulke and MacArthur, were summoned and an express despatched for Dr Hume, the Duke's personal physician, in London.

This was the beginning of a serious attack which everyone thought would at least end in impaired faculties, if not in loss of life. The local doctor, MacArthur, diagnosed 'an affection of the stomach exhausted by two days of almost complete inanition, added to a long ride on a cold bleak day'. He also commented on the fact that for several months past the Duke had 'generally pursued a system of starving – eating seldom and very sparingly'.

The servants confirmed the fact that on the day of the seizure the Duke had eaten only dry bread with a cup of tea for breakfast and had foregone luncheon as was his habit. At dinner the previous evening the Duke had spent a few minutes only at table, picking at his food with a fork while keeping his right hand in his pocket.

It was unfortunate that the Duke was alone when he was taken ill – his eldest son was in Scotland; the youngest in Canada; his brother, Lord Maryborough, was in London, and even Arbuthnot was absent. Yet he lacked nothing in warmth or devotion from his servants, kindly noted Lord Mahon.

A large dinner party for officers of the garrison had been planned for that evening. Captain Watts, standing at the foot of the bed where the Duke lay motionless, suggested to Lord Mahon that a message ought to be sent cancelling the event. At this, the Duke opened his eyes and painfully whispered: 'I desire that the dinner fixed for today may go on; and I beg Colonel Thompson, Colonel Morris and Captain Watts will be so good as to receive the officers.'

The Duke passed a bad night but seemed easier on the following morning. At about 2.30 in the afternoon, Dr Hume arrived and Lord Maryborough, who had just returned to Deal Castle, rode over anxious to consult with him. The following day the Duke was not nearly so good and the doctors feared a fever coming on even though the Duke himself appeared cheerful and was adamant that the worst was over.

This idea he proceeded to demonstrate. He rose and dressed unaided, read all his letters and wrote replies. 'No less,' despaired Lord Mahon, 'than seven or eight in his writing went in tonight's post.' Next day he felt stronger, wrote several more letters, paid his bills, regulated his household affairs and arranged for a sum of money to be distributed during the winter quarter among the poor of Walmer.

It had, in any case, been thought advisable that the Duke return to London as soon as possible to be under the supervision of his doctors there and so on the Friday morning he prepared to depart. His carriage was brought round to the drawbridge and when he departed, as was the custom, the gigantic Union Jack was struck from the tower. Naturally. he did not forget to say farewell to his little friends, the Wilton children, and he stopped his carriage at their corner house in Walmer village. The children could not bear to part from him, having 'received so many kindnesses from him, and bore him so much attachment', their governess later confided to Lord Mahon. Every time he made for the door, they ran ahead of him and barred his way!

Eventually the Duke entered his britzka and drove himself to London – a journey of eight hours – where he was due to attend the Privy Council at which Queen Victoria would announce her forthcoming marriage to Prince Albert.

The arrival of Prince Albert at Dover in 1839 prior to his marriage with Queen Victoria

Chapter Four

QUEEN VICTORIA'S HOLIDAY

QUEEN VICTORIA expressed her desire to borrow Walmer Castle for her seaside holiday in the autumn of 1842 since an outbreak of scarlet fever had rendered her intended use of Brighton Pavilion inadvisable. The Queen, in any case, despised this garish Regency building set in a brash seaside resort where the people were 'indiscreet and troublesome'.

The suggestion regarding Walmer Castle had come originally from the Prime Minister, Sir Robert Peel. Here is the Duke's reply:

Walmer Castle
26 October

My Dear Peel,

Arbuthnot has shown me your letter to him respecting this house. Nothing can be more convenient to me than to place it at Her Majesty's disposition any time she pleases.

I am only apprehensive that the accommodation of the castle would be scarcely sufficient for Her Majesty, The Prince and the Royal children and such suite as must attend.

It is the most delightful seaside residence to be found, anywhere, particularly for children. They can be out all day on the ramparts, and platforms quite dry, and the beautiful gardens and wood are enclosed and sheltered from the severe gales of wind. There are good lodgings at Walmer village and at Walmer Beach at no great distance from the Castle, not above half a mile.

(It should be remembered the Queen was not at that time enamoured by the Duke for it was only in later years that their acquaintance developed into true admiration and friendship.)

Immediately, Mr Hardwick, an architect, was despatched from London to

Queen Victoria in 1842

make the appropriate improvements to Walmer Castle in anticipation of the royal visit. And so began a frantic programme of 'knocking up and knocking down in all directions' for the greater comfort of the Duke's guests. Pitt's room was hastily partitioned off and gaily papered to form a pleasant dining room; the Duke's library was emptied of its contents and turned into twin dressing rooms; the dining room and an adjoining bedroom were thrown into one to make a spacious dormitory for the royal couple while a window was knocked into the thick walls to enable Her Majesty to have a view southwards of the Downs. Lastly, the village carpenter was employed to put up a little shelf to hold a time-piece in view of the royal bed – a tiny detail understood to be essential for Prince Albert's complete happiness.

A dramatic entrance hall had been created at the fortress to welcome the royal guests. The long, dark passageway linking the archway over the drawbridge and the principal entrance to the castle had been enclosed by a striped awning to resemble an Indian pavilion. The interior was furnished with trophies captured by the Duke of Wellington during the storming of Seringapatam in Southern India in 1799 when he defeated the local leader, Tippoo Sahib, Napoleon's fanatical ally, known as the 'Tiger of Mysore'.

A detachment of 130 Grenadier Guards under Colonel Paget was sent ahead to Walmer Castle to act as a guard of honour during the Queen's stay and was quartered at Deal Barracks. Important guests were to be lodged in grand houses along Walmer foreshore.

And as the great day approached their attentive host gave precise directions in his nearly illegible handwriting for Her Majesty's reception:

Ship Hotel, Dover.
Nov. 9th '42

My dear Capt Watts,

The Queen will be at Walmer Castle on tomorrow at three or at four o'clock.

I beg you to recollect that the Royal Salute may be practised(?) by the time that H.M. will reach Upper Deal Mill.

There should be a Guard of Honour in readiness if the weather chart be fine and not raining. It might parade in the field at a distance from the Road & the Castle; so as not to frighten the Queen's Horses.

In case a permanent Guard should be required while the Queen shall be at Walmer Castle the Laundry must be occupied as a Guard Room.

My Mangle and other Laundry furniture must be moved out; into the Stables or the Coach House, if as is probable the Queen should require the Stables and the Coach House Lord Charles will let you know: as also whether a Sergeant's or a Corporal's Guard shall mount(?) daily.

The Police are to occupy the Rooms over the Laundry; Heretofore occupied by my kitchen(?) servants.

You must get the Barracks Master to send to the Laundry three Barrack beds by way of Guard Bed(s) and a Table.

Yours truely,
Wellington

P.S. I shall be at Walmer Castle tomorrow morning.

Captain Watts was further reminded to hoist the Royal Standard upon Her Majesty's arrival at Walmer Castle. Meanwhile, the Duke himself retreated to Dover. . .

*

The Duke of Wellington greeting Queen Victoria on the outskirts of Sandwich

Finally, the great day came. On Thursday, 10 November the royal family left Windsor, travelled to Paddington by train and then journeyed through Kent in a procession consisting of three carriages and four escorted by light cavalry. Queen Victoria and Prince Albert were accompanied by their young children: Prince Albert Edward, the Prince of Wales, and Princess Victoria, the Princess Royal.

The illustrious company included the Dowager Lady Lyttleton, recently appointed royal governess; Lady Portman, the Lady in Waiting; Viscount Sydney, the Lord in Waiting; and Lord Charles Wellesley, the Equerry in Waiting on Prince Albert. The Honourable C. A. Murray, Master of the

Household, plus several other members of the royal suite, had arrived at the castle in advance.

The royal party proceeded at a 'rapid pace' across Kent, halting briefly to change horses and escorts at the Green Man Hotel, Blackheath, and the Fountain Inn, Canterbury. They travelled along the Dover Road – Shooter's Hill, Dartford, Rochester, Chatham, Sittingbourne and Canterbury. It was the same route Prince Albert had travelled in reverse nearly three years previously when he came to marry Victoria.

Everywhere, the royal party was greeted by loyal citizens anxious to express their devotion but the Queen had given strict instructions that their journey was not to be unduly delayed as she was desirous of reaching Walmer that same evening. Her Majesty directed the royal nurses, however, to sit on opposite sides of the carriage so that people lining the route might see one of the royal infants, either Vicky or Bertie.

The Prince of Wales and the Princess Royal

When the procession, which consisted of three carriages preceded by a troop of the 7th Hussars stationed at Canterbury and a guard of honour provided by the 51st Infantry, reached Sholden, on the outskirts of Deal, they passed under a triumphal arch to be greeted by a procession of eminent townsfolk. The reception party had gathered at the town hall in the afternoon and marched to Upper Deal in the following order:

Numerous boatmen bearing the flags of all nations preceded by the royal standard;
Children of the Deal Charity Schools, two by two;
Band of music;
The mace bearer;
The Mayor;
The Revd Mr Backhouse;
Aldermen of the borough;
Town councillors;
The inhabitants of Deal, consisting of several hundred, four deep;
The Deal pilots;
The Deal boatmen.

At Deal the occasion was observed as a general holiday, every shop being closed, in order to give 'all classes and persons' an opportunity of receiving their beloved sovereign. Upwards of one thousand townsfolk had turned out to greet Her Majesty including officers of the Navy Yard, officers of the Custom House and the whole of the fellowship of pilots. Local boatmen stationed themselves in groups of six along the planned route to the castle, every other man bearing alternately a flag or a torch.

Queen Victoria's drive through Deal to Walmer Castle was reported in *The Illustrated London News* (19 November 1842) :

Nothing could exceed the joyous welcome given to Her Majesty and His Royal Highness by the loyal inhabitants of this part of the country, who had assembled from the neighbouring towns and villages for several miles around. There was scarcely a house but what exhibited some appropriate emblem or device. The royal ensign, flags of every hue and nation, were suspended from the public buildings, across the streets, and from the windows of many of the principal houses; and the vessels along the coast were also decked out in their gayest colours.

Precisely at four o'clock the Queen arrived at the castle 'in excellent health and spirits' where she was welcomed by the Duke of Wellington. Immediately the royal salute was fired by the guard of honour and the troops, and this was repeated by eight guns on the upper and six on the lower rampart. The journey of 103 miles had been achieved in nine hours, with only two stops of a quarter of an hour each to change horses. 'It was very fatiguing,' complained Lady Lyttleton, 'owing to immense crowds, continual cheers and excitement of wreaths and bonfires, and triumphal arches, church bells and cannons all the way. . .'

Queen Victoria's bedroom at Walmer, photographed at the turn of the century (Country Life)

Confusion reigned inside the castle. Earlier in the day when the Duke had ridden over from Dover to inspect the arrangements for the Queen's arrival preparations were even at that late hour nowhere near complete. Now trunks and baggages belonging to gentlemen of the entourage who were to lodge in houses along The Beach were piled high on the passages and staircases. Servants, maids and nurses flew about on their various errands so that the Duke had difficulty in escorting Her Majesty to her apartments in the dark. Courteously, the Duke waited until all the luggage had been sorted out and the Queen comfortably settled before he retired – thankfully – to Dover.

There he wrote an account of the day's excitement to Lady Wilton:

Ship Hotel, Dover.
11 November

I came down here on Wednesday and went over to Walmer Castle yesterday morning, to see what the House was likely to turn out after having been pulled to Pieces. It looked very little promising or likely to be ready by four o'clock, at which Hour I expected that The Queen would arrive. I then went over to Sandwich to meet Her Majesty upon the frontier of my Jurisdiction. I had intended to meet her on horseback, as I had last year in Hampshire. But it rained so hard that I thought it impossible I should be able to ride, and did not take my Horses. I waited some Hours at Sandwich, when Lord Fitzroy Somerset arrived with some Horses of Lord Maryborough's; and I mounted one of them in a moment of Interval between the Showers, and rode out towards Ash to meet Her Majesty; which I did just before dark. She asked me into Her Carriage; but I declined saying that I wished to receive Her Majesty in Walmer Castle, and that I had my own carriage ready at Sandwich. Accordingly I rode before Her Carriage into Sandwich, and set off, and reached Walmer Castle ten minutes before Her Majesty did. Her Postillions (Her own) drove Her very badly into the Gate of the Tower. She stuck in it, and was obliged to get out of the Carriage. I believe that the Children were carried over the Bridge. . .

She did not arrive till after dark which made the Confusion greater. However, the old living apartments and Her Bed Room and Prince Albert's had been but little touched and, as soon as the Trunks & co could be got

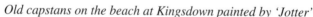

Old capstans on the beach at Kingsdown painted by 'Jotter'

out of the Way, would have been comfortable enough. She had asked me to dine and sleep there last night, which I had declined, as I had really so much to do here that I could not stay. I came off here consequently before the House was put in order. I have heard no more since. . .

*

Soon after their arrival, the Queen and Prince Albert did what every visitor to the coast does – they went to look at the sea. Offshore lay three revenue cutters – *The Ranger, Lady Flora* and *Sea Lark* – with their masts and rigging brilliantly illuminated. Numerous rockets were fired by these ships in the course of the evening in addition to those discharged from the Pilot House in Beach Street at Deal. As the wind was rather rough Victoria and Albert stayed for a few minutes only before returning to the castle to sit down to dinner. That night the royal circle was confined to the distinguished personages who had accompanied Her Majesty and His Royal Highness from London.

One member of the royal party remained decidedly unimpressed by her new surroundings. Sarah, Lady Lyttleton, continued her jaundiced account of the expedition in her diary (11 November):

This is much what I expected. A big round tower, with additions stuck on. Immense thick walls, and a heap of conical rooms of the odd shape necessary as parts of a round house, built close upon the shingly beach. . . It seems needless to go out for air, doors and windows all chatter and sing at once, and hardly keep out the dark storm of wind and rain which is howling round. . .

*

At sunrise on Friday morning the royal standard was hoisted on the tower at Walmer Castle announcing the presence of Her Majesty Queen Victoria. At nine o'clock, the *Thunderer*, a line-of-battle ship under the command of Captain Pring, manned the yards and saluted the sovereign with a discharge of twenty-one guns.

The Queen and Prince Albert rose at their usual hour and breakfasted at half-past eight. An hour later the couple took a brisk stroll along Walmer Beach, unattended, in spite of a stiff gale blowing south-south-west. Several heavy showers came on in the afternoon preventing them from taking a planned carriage ride.

The addresses of the mayor and other authorities of Deal were forwarded to Her Majesty and during the course of the day many of the gentry residing in the neighbourhood left their calling cards at the castle. The royal dinner party in the evening was again very select it being Her Majesty's expressed wish to be as retiring as possible during her stay at Walmer.

On Saturday morning, soon after ten o'clock, the Queen and Prince Albert left the castle and walked upwards of an hour unattended along the beach. Although the wind was 'blowing great guns', Her Majesty appeared in high spirits and delighted in the animated seascape where several hundred sailing vessels sought shelter in the Downs.

The royal couple were strolling in the direction of Deal when a sudden rain storm came on and they made a hasty retreat to the castle. But before they had time to reach home the sun again appeared and shone brightly so they extended their walk towards Kingsdown Cliffs.

The Queen and Prince Albert drove through Walmer on several occasions and the streets were decorated with flags to welcome them

During their walk a poor man with a strange dog, rescued a few weeks previously from the wreck of a Russian timber ship, was accosted by the Queen. Her Majesty desired to know what kind of animal it was. At midday they returned to the castle.

That afternoon the sun shone brilliantly. Her Majesty's carriage and four with outriders was ordered to be in attendance at the castle for a quarter past three. A slight shower, however, delayed the Queen's departure for almost half an hour. When Her Majesty stepped into the open carriage attended by Lady Portman she was cheered by a large crowd of inhabitants who had gathered at the castle gates. Prince Albert accompanied the Queen on horseback.

The royal procession travelled along the Walmer Road proceeding through

Prospect Place (Victoria Road) and Lower Street (now High Street) along St. George's Place through West Street to Upper Deal. They returned to Walmer Castle via the top road past the water tower and into Walmer village.

Afterwards this indefatigable couple walked a considerable distance along the Strand but the wind was so strong that it was with the greatest difficulty that the Queen could stay upright!

They returned to the castle and Prince Albert continued his walk in the company of Colonel Murray. Her Majesty, attended by Viscount Sydney and Lady Portman, spent some time studying the pictures in the castle gallery.

*

Violence of the wind had prevented either of the French mail packets from entering Dover Harbour. Shortly before nine o'clock they were seen in company with a French passage boat beating their way up Channel towards Deal. There, after laying-to for some time, the bags were landed by local boatmen. Her Majesty, who had been at breakfast when the mails passed, sent out to Captain Lane, the superintending governor of the castle, to learn their name and destination.

During the gale a French fishing boat of considerable burden brought-to at a very short distance from the shore opposite Walmer Castle. Its extraordinary appearance attracted the attention of Queen Victoria and so the character of the vessel was carefully explained to her. The French captain's infringement of the three mile limit was considered of great impudence, particularly when it was so clearly under the observation of the English sovereign.

The *Thunderer* was still lying-off but the fierce wind obliged Captain Pring to keep her 'taut' and the top gallant masts which had been lowered on Friday had not again been raised.

Rumours reached Walmer Castle that seven Deal boatmen were drowned by the upsetting of their craft a few miles from the shore. They were signalled that morning to go on board a Lisbon steamer, weather-bound in the roads, and it was feared that the rolling of the vessel capsized their boat. Oars had been washed ashore and a boat was spotted floating upside down in the Downs.

*

All day on Sunday the boisterous weather continued preventing the Queen and the royal infants from leaving Walmer Castle. Her Majesty did, however, take brief turns about the ramparts in between showers. At midday the whole of the royal party assembled in the large drawing-room which had been furnished as a private chapel. Divine service was then conducted by the Revd Henry William Wilberforce, Perpetual Curate of Old Saint Mary's Church at Walmer. Mr Wilberforce was the youngest son of the illustrious William Wilberforce who abolished the slave trade. He preached an apt sermon – considering the adverse weather – 'For as the lightning cometh out of the east . . . so shall the coming of the Son of Man be' – Matthew 24 v. 27. (Less appropriately, considering the present company, this passage continues: 'For wheresoever the carcass is there shall the eagles be gathered together.')

Between three and four o'clock in the afternoon, Prince Albert, attended by the Hon. C. A. Murray, walked for half an hour on the beach, despite torrential rain. The gentry continued to call at the castle to pay their respects: Sir Edward Knatchbull; Mr Edward Rice of Dane Court, Tilmanstone; Admiral Brown and Captain Harvey in addition to mayors of neighbouring towns. That evening the royal dinner party for the first time was extended to include local gentry.

*

At around eight o'clock that evening the wind shifted into the west-north-west and in the course of the night the wind became calm. On the Monday morning Her Majesty was greeted with the spectacle of upwards of one hundred sail lying at anchor in the Downs. The Queen and Prince Albert strolled along the shore for a considerable time and the royal children were taken out for an airing by their nurses and attendants.

At midday Prince Albert went on board the *Thunderer*. He was steered there by Captain Westbrook of the Coastguard in his galley. Attended by Colonel Wylde and a certain Dr Praetorius, the Prince remained on board for almost an hour inspecting the design of this admirable vessel. The visit had been unannounced and Captain Pring and Captain Bullock, who were ashore, instantly put off to attend the Prince. On landing, Prince Albert was saluted by Sir William Curtis' yacht, which was anchored opposite the castle. Captain Bullock's steamer, *Fearless*, also dressed her colours.

Queen Victoria decided on an impulse to visit Dover Castle that afternoon and an express was sent to the Governor, Colonel Jenkinson, to warn him of Her Majesty's imminent arrival. The Queen and Prince Albert enjoyed their tour of inspection, examining every object of interest and admiring the views from the towers. Afterwards they were driven in an open carriage attended by outriders into the town and along the seafront.

Although the townsfolk could have had no intimation of the royal visit, they had naturally been on the alert expecting that this honour would be paid them on the first fine day. Consequently the streets were thronged with cheering crowds as the procession passed.

The author of *Rambling Recollections of the Neighbourhood of Dover* (1848) humorously pictured the scene:

At this time Castle Hill was all alive, ladies who heretofore were seen moving as stately as swans upon a lake were running about in all

The Cinque Port of Dover (The Print Room, Deal)

directions, many of them scrambling from the new into the old road, cutting off corners to take up a second or third position to look again at their beloved Queen. . .

The Constable's Gateway at Dover Castle (The Print Room, Deal)

This visit did not terminate until the royal party had been round the pier, as far as the carriage road would allow. The pace travelled was rather slow, and the royal carriage was followed by two or three flies, a donkey chaise bringing up the rear. This was merely a circumstance; the vehicles travelling the same road naturally fell in behind, still they formed a sort of procession, and nothing short of genuine royalty could have stood it, but it did so well, and the visit terminated to the satisfaction of all!'

That evening the whole town was illuminated to celebrate the joyous event.

Transparencies 'of the most loyal description' were exhibited in every window and on the premises of a certain Mr Bennett at the corner of Bench Street was displayed the royal cypher surmounted by a star depicted in brilliant gas lighting.

Yet the day was tinged with anxiety concerning the fate of the crew of the Deal galley which had been lost during the severe gale the previous afternoon. Incredibly, information was received about seven o'clock in the evening that every man had been saved through the brave efforts of those on board the Lisbon vessel. News was immediately conveyed to Walmer Castle.

Queen Victoria was overjoyed and sent to Deal the following day to ascertain the circumstances regarding the unfortunate boatmen who had lost their craft – and very nearly their lives – in their attempt to reach the stricken steamer. Generously, Her Majesty donated twenty pounds towards the purchase of a new boat. That morning there had been a recurrence of the weekend's stormy weather: a tempestuous gale with pelting rain and a south-easterly wind.

*

On Wednesday morning at eight o'clock the *Hyacinth*, an 18-gun sloop, London bound from the West Indies, entered the Downs and dropped anchor abreast of Walmer Castle. On the instant her sails were furled and her yards manned – as if by magic! She then fired a royal salute . . . up anchor . . . set sail in a trice and proceeded – under the pressure of a stiffish breeze and at a rapid rate – towards the River Thames. The royal couple watched this spectacle from the window of their breakfast room.

At half-past nine, Queen Victoria and Prince Albert slipped out through a wicket gate in the castle grounds unnoticed by members of the public and set off for a stroll in the direction of Kingsdown. They were unaccompanied apart from three Scots terriers and one of the Prince's hounds. Halfway there a sudden squall of rain compelled them to seek shelter in a boathouse which, beside being a store for nautical gear, was also the home of an elderly boatman, Thomas Erridge. The Queen and the Prince were offered an improvised seat – spars placed across upturned water casks hastily covered with sailcloth – and they chatted freely with the humble fisherman and his wife. The Queen asked their daughter, Rachel, if she knew what vessel had just anchored in the Downs and she smiled at her mistaken reply that she supposed it was a French frigate. The rude but kindly hospitality of this simple family greatly impressed Her Majesty for she later rewarded them with a pension. The royal couple continued their journey to Kingsdown, climbed the cliffs and circled an ancient landmark on the summit. On this occasion the distance covered was about two miles and the tracks were quite rough in places. Queen Victoria was a rapid walker and she had no objection to traversing a ploughed field when she encountered one!

Her Majesty returned to the castle 'the very picture of blooming health, her colour being wonderfully heightened by the exercise and the healthful breeze of easterly wind that blew right in her face as she approached the castle. . .' (according to a reporter for *The Illustrated London News*). Certainly the adventure had done them both good. In the afternoon they repeated it!

There was a hearty meal awaiting them that evening. 'Covers were laid at the castle for twelve,' informed the reporter, 'being three over the usual number of the royal dinner party.'

Although the weather remained adverse, the Queen continued to enjoy her marine resort exceedingly. As for Prince Albert, he revelled in it. Blow high, blow low . . . wet or dry . . . he determined to explore the coastline and he delighted in the invigorating salt sea air.

Lady Lyttleton noted with amusement this sudden interest in nautical affairs:

We have, I begin to notice, rather a raised tone of conversation of late – many bits of information and naval matters, and scientific subjects come up and are talked of very pleasantly at dinner. The Prince and the Queen are reading Hallam's *Constitutional History of England* together, most carefully, and for a light book, *St Simon's Memoirs*. Very pleasant to find him reading loud to her, while she was at cross-stitch, as I did the other evening before dressing time. Oh! what a mine of blessings is that 'Love rules the court' as he does! What a mine of blessings there is, all sent thro' those potent blue eyes!

On the Saturday of the second week of her holiday Queen Victoria succumbed to the castle draughts and caught a chill. Attempts had been made to warm the passageways by means of hot air blown through pipes leading from a stove 'of a peculiar construction' concealed in the castle grounds. Sir James Clark, the Queen's physician, was consulted immediately. He prescribed a gargle ('decoction of papaver') a soothing draught ('sodium bicarbonate, tincture of colchicum, tincture of hyoscyamus with a compound tincture of camphor') and a mystifying ointment containing green hellebore to be freshly made up in the town and sent to the castle. Her Majesty was not confined indoors, however, for she spent several hours walking on the beach that Sunday. Divine service was performed at the castle by the Revd Charles Lane, Rector of St Leonard's Church, Deal.

*

Monday was the second birthday of Princess Victoria, the Princess Royal. The people of Deal were determined to arrange a day of celebration which the royal infant would always remember. At daybreak the *Thunderer*, plus another of Her Majesty's ships which had come in to the Downs that morning, dressed their colours and fired a royal salute. Three gunboats from the *Thunderer* came in close to the castle and fired similar volleys. About ten o'clock the town band drew up on the meadow in front of the castle and played the National Anthem followed by a selection of popular airs. Almost the entire population of Deal turned out to greet the young princess and stood before the castle cheering wildly.

A regatta was held by the local boatmen to celebrate the Princess Royal's birthday

Lady Lyttleton billed and cooed over her charge:

Princessy was most funny all day, joining in the cheers, and desiring to be lifted up to look at the people, to whom she bowed very actively, whether they were in sight or not. . . She was prodigiously dressed up in garter-blue velvet, Brussels lace, white shoes, pearls and diamonds and looked too comical.

It was an uncommonly fine day, with the wind colouring a brisk gale and the sun shone brilliantly. Capital sailing weather! Everything favoured the Deal and Walmer boatmen who had organised an impromptu regatta in honour of the Princess Royal.

The Illustrated London News reported the occasion:

The boats to the number of thirty, with every inch of canvas they could carry, ran down from Deal under the castle walls. Here they braced up, and proceeded to sea, standing out to westward till they had measured some three miles towards the South Sand Light. They then turned in on the other tack till they came close under Walmer Castle, where they drew up, and each man standing up in his boat, off hats, and gave three or more hearty

79

British cheers that resounded for many miles. At this time Her Majesty, Prince Albert and suite, were on the ramparts witnessing the interesting spectacle, and both the Queen and the Prince most graciously condescended to acknowledge the devotion of the brave and hearty boatmen of Deal by repeatedly bowing. The band then struck up a national air and the loyal fleet again stretched out seaward, rounded the *Thunderer* and about 12 o'clock returned to Deal in beautiful order, after having traversed some twelve miles in something less than two hours.

Immediately after their return to the shore, the boatmen were summoned to the Town Hall by the Mayor of Deal, Edward Darby. Proudly he read aloud two letters he had received from the Lord in Waiting congratulating the boatmen on their display. Then he invited the boatmen, who numbered above four hundred, to 'splice the mainbrace' (drink a tot of rum!) to toast the health of the royal visitors.

During the afternoon, the gunboats of the *Thunderer* organised a sham fight between that vessel and the shore. George Leith, recently retired captain of Walmer Castle, entertained the town band to dinner. The Queen, now deeply concerned with matters nautical, commanded Mr Charles Wootton, Superintendent of the Navy Yard, to supply her with a list of every warship passing through the English Channel.

In the evening the whole town was illuminated upon a grand scale. Her Majesty's ship, *Thunderer*, commenced the display at six o'clock by opening her upper and lower deck ports to reveal brilliant lights. Twenty minutes later she fired two signal guns. At this the firework display began in earnest. Blue lights were displayed on every mast so that from the shore they appeared as one spectacular blaze of fire. Marines on the quarter-deck fired a 'feu de joie' amid a hail of rockets. Finally the *Thunderer* terminated her part of the display by firing a royal salute from her 36-pounders.

Next, the *Fearless* steamer, the *Lady Flora* and the revenue cutter, *Sealark*, anchored to the westward of the *Thunderer*, close under the castle, and began firing rockets and large Roman candles which had the effect of illuminating the castle and surrounding seashore. The evening, which was remarkably fine, enabled Her Majesty to watch the events from the castle ramparts.

*

On each fine day the Prince of Wales and the Princess Royal were driven in a small chaise along the beach at Walmer 'enjoying the sea breezes and the delightful weather'.

During the whole of their stay, Mr Hulke, the eminent physician from Deal, attended Walmer Castle at eight o'clock each morning to ensure the well-being of the royal infants. On Friday 11 November he was introduced by Sir James

Clarke, the Queen's personal physician, to Lady Lyttleton, the children's governess. He was informed of the times and contents of the nursery meals and – ominously – shown the medicine chest. For these attendances, Mr Hulke received a fee of £45 from Prince Albert. Mr Hulke kept a careful record of his daily visits:

12 Friday: Went to the Castle at quarter past eight – was announced to Lady Lyttleton and introduced to the Prince of Wales – the Princess Royal – both children are healthy altho' looking rather pale.

13 Sunday: Visited the royal infants at the same hour – both well – Lady Lyttleton complained of a slight cold.

14 Monday: the Princess Royal seemed slightly oppressed – gave her . . . a powder – the Prince quite well.

15 Tuesday: the Princess Royal seemed quite well – but a slight wheezing sometimes manifested itself – to have a powder in the morning – a warm bath at night. Dr MacArthur saw her.

16 Wednesday: the Princess Royal passed a good night – took her breakfast very well – the Prince has his diet slightly altered. Arrowroot – the bowels being a little relaxed – this morning quite well.

17 Thursday: the Prince of Wales quite well – the Princess Royal has a small red spot on the cheek – the eye tooth on that side not quite free from the Gum – used the gum lancet

*

On the morning of Monday 21 November – the birthday of the Princess Royal – Mr Hulke was half-an-hour late for his appointment. He apologised to Lady Lyttleton and explained that his wife had just given birth to a son. When the Queen heard this news she was delighted and commanded that the infant should be named 'Victor' in honour of the Princess Royal. (Victor Hulke was, in fact, the seventh son and thirteenth child.)

The next day when Mr Hulke appeared – precisely on time – at the castle Princess Victoria handed him a gold pencil in a presentation case decorated with precious stones as a gift for her tiny namesake. (Apparently this had been a present to the Queen from her husband so it was also of sentimental value.) The royal gift – a tiny gold propelling pencil bearing medallion portraits of Queen Victoria and Prince Albert – remains today with the Hulke family in Canada.

The gold propelling pencil presented to Mr Hulke's new-born son by the Princess Royal (Sydney Hulke)

81

For the Wednesday, a tour of the *Thunderer* was planned but an outbreak of smallpox among the crew rendered the visit inadvisable. Instead, a cruise was organised for the royal party aboard the revenue cutter, *Lady Flora*.

Prince Albert preferred to attend the meet of the Beachborough hounds at Betteshanger Gorse. There was a 'brilliant field' composed of more than three hundred gentry and yeomanry from the surrounding neighbourhood. *The Illustrated London News* again gave full coverage:

> At half-past eleven o'clock His Royal Highness Prince Albert, attended by Lord Charles Wellesley, the Hon. C. A. Murray and Col. Wylde, arrived on the field. After about ten minutes draw in the furze, a dog fox was started, which, with much difficulty, was made to break cover, when he ran for Betteshanger Park, the estate of Frederick Morrice, Esq., and got into a small plantation near the house. This caused a check for about twenty minutes in consequence of the fox being frequently headed back by so large a field. At last he broke away into the open country, and the field at this time was exceedingly animate. It, however, lasted but a very short time, as he was run into and killed near Eastry turnpike, after indifferent running of about twenty minutes. The Prince being well up at the death, was presented with the brush by Mr Brockman, who hunted the pack.

Later in the day another fox was started at Knowlton Park and this was killed at Betteshanger Gorse after a run of twenty-five minutes.

The Queen and Prince Albert made an excursion together to Ramsgate on the Thursday. Escorted by the Deputy Chairman of the Harbour Trustees, Sir W. Curtis, Her Majesty walked the length of the East Pier where she watched the arrival of four vessels in the harbour. One of these, a brig, very nearly struck the stonework and had a narrow escape! Afterwards, the Queen witnessed the launching of a Genoese vessel, *Felice*, from the patent slipway. Refreshment was then served in the Pier House. Afterwards an audience was given to the

Ramsgate Harbour (The Print Room, Deal)

officers of the *Compte de Flandres*, a Belgian brig-of-war berthed in Ramsgate Harbour.

Another walk along the beach at Walmer for the royal couple on Friday – 'as far as Herridge's hut and back' – after which the weather became so unfavourable as to prevent their leaving the castle again that day.

*

Prince Albert

Adverse weather conditions over the weekend confined the royal party once more to the castle while ships in the Dover Strait struggled against the gales. The French mail packet, *Courier*, failed to make Dover Harbour. Instead she came into the Downs to put her mails ashore at Deal although her passengers were compelled to remain on board overnight until they could be landed in safety at Ramsgate Harbour.

The Revd Montague Pennington, Perpetual Curate of Saint George's Church, Deal, hastily prepared a sermon which he delivered before the royal family at the castle on that third Sunday. The Queen remained within the castle all that day although she seems to have completely recovered from her cold.

The Queen had splendid views from the castle windows, however, to hold her attention. Hundreds of vessels were now at anchor in the Downs in consequence of strong south-westerly winds and the continental steamers were again unable to land the mails at Dover. About this time a report was received that a wandering lunatic who regarded himself as Napoleon III called at the castle and demanded admission.

National news of great importance was conveyed to the Queen at the castle during her seaside holiday. Her Majesty was informed that – after a defeat in the Opium Wars – China had ceded a large barren rock at the mouth of the Pearl River: Hong Kong. This opened the ports of Canton, Amoy, Foochow, Ningpo and Shanghai to British trade.

*

Prince Albert took the opportunity during that final week to explore the Kent coast. On Tuesday 29 November, he rode with Colonel Wylde to St Margaret's Bay to inspect the lighthouse then in the course of construction on the South Foreland. On Wednesday 30 November, he was taken out to inspect Captain Bullock's Beacon on the Goodwin Sands.

The South Foreland Lighthouse

The Prince had some time before expressed his desire to inspect the refuge beacon erected by Captain Bullock on the Goodwins in 1840 and he seized the opportunity offered by a calm day to venture out into the Channel. Leaving the beach at Deal about noon in the four-oared gig belonging to the *Fearless*, which was steered by Captain Bullock himself, Prince Albert began by inspecting the *Wasp*, a sixteen-gun brig commanded by Captain Drew. As the Prince had never before been on board an English brig-of-war he was astonished at the confined nature of the officers' berths and the cramped accommodation of the crew. After touring the brig, the Prince proceeded at once on board the *Fearless* which was about to convey fresh food and water to the beacon. Forthwith this ship steamed out to the beacon which lay between the North and South Goodwins in an area known as Trinity Bay. On the way they passed a large number of outward bound vessels thought to have been in the region of one hundred sail. Although the state of the tide would not allow a close examination of the refuge, they remained in the vicinity for almost half an hour. The Prince was greatly interested to learn from Captain Bullock minute details concerning its construction.

Captain Bullock's Beacon had been erected on the Goodwins on Thursday 10 September 1840 with the assistance of Captain Boys, Superintendent of the Navy Yard at Deal. This remarkable invention was described by Captain Bullock thus:

The shaft or mast (40 feet in height and 12 feet in diameter) is sunk into the sand, through a strong frame of oak, in the form of a cross, firmly secured by four bars of iron and laden with several tons of ballast. . . On the shaft is fitted an octagon gallery, capable of holding 30 or 40 persons, and never less than sixteen feet above high water mark. Beneath this gallery there is a temporary safety for 20 persons or more.

The mast is also fitted with a light top mast on which a blue flag (always at hand) can be hoisted as a signal when aid is required from the shore. . . Blue was fixed upon for the colour of the flag as being supposed to be visible at a great distance. Directions how to proceed to those persons who may fortunately succeed in reaching the safety beacon are given in eight languages, and bread and water with a small supply of spirits are always left upon the beacon properly protected from the weather.

To the beacon is always apprehended a chain ladder of easy ascent, as well as cleets to the mast, and a large basket chair is kept in readiness, with ropes and blocks to aid and secure the exhausted. The sides of the gallery are fitted with sail cloth reefed all round it, which could be unrolled and made fast to the flagstaff if required, the object being to protect with a temporary shelter any shipwrecked sailors who might reach the gallery.

As the Goodwins are partly dry at low water to a great extent, and as vessels which strike them seldom go to pieces in a single tide, the

probability is that some of the wrecked crew would be enabled to reach the sand during the interval, and the safety beacon would then become their only refuge.

This first beacon remained in place until 6 August 1844 when it was partially destroyed by a Dutch galliot colliding with it. A second beacon replaced the original structure but this disappeared in the severe winter of 1847.

*

Preparations had been made hastily for the departure of the royal holidaymakers on Saturday 3 December. (The Queen was most careful to avoid travelling on Sundays.) The journey to London was once more effected by road since the South Eastern Railway had not progressed far beyond Ashford. Train travel was, in any case, still a novelty for the royal family since they had made their first journey by rail from Slough to Paddington earlier that year. The Grenadiers marched to Margate and took a steamer for London while the *Thunderer* proceeded westward. Queen Victoria, as a parting gift, donated one hundred pounds towards Deal charities.

Lady Lyttleton was delighted to be ensconced once more at Windsor Castle. The return journey to London had been comparatively smooth: 'one gallop from Walmer to London, and a railroad rush hither', she conceded in her diary (4 December). There had been the same confusion over baggage as on the outward journey, she lamented; 'night things, playthings, rusks, shawls' all tiresomely strayed in that veritable 'nursery on wheels'. But now she could relax and 'enjoy the great luxury of a nice fire and drawn curtains . . . and my regular fine dinner'.

Queen Victoria's and Prince Albert's holiday at Walmer Castle appeared to the locals at least to have been a resounding success. There was speculation that their holiday in Kent would become an annual event 'on account of the purity of its air, and the natural beauty of its scenery'. Indeed, the royal visit seems to have excited the most delusive speculation, for *The Illustrated London News* reported on an ambitious project to build a vast estate of detached houses connected by a long esplanade with separate gardens and suitable offices along the foreshore. The plan was to turn this sleepy port into a fashionable watering-place to rival Brighton.

Fortunately the scheme came to nothing – it could have ruined Walmer. And, in any case, Sir James Clark rather put a damper on the idea of the Queen's holiday in Kent becoming a regular occurrence when he confided to his colleague, William Hulke: 'They went late this year; the weather was bad; they all caught colds, and fancy the climate was not good.'

Opposite – Captain Bullock's Beacon on the Goodwin Sands (Margate Library Local Studies Collection)

A postcard of Queen Victoria's bedroom showing contemporary items of furniture and alterations to the tester bed

*

The Queen's bedroom on the south side of Walmer Castle contains very little furniture from the time of her visit. Even the mahogany four-post bed was drastically altered by later Lords Warden – which is why modern visitors express surprise as to how small it is! Lady Granville confessed in a letter to Lord Curzon: 'We were Goths enough to cut it down to a half tester, but must plead as an excuse that it was a hideous object with curtains and deep valance and canopy, all in yellow moreen with a woollen fringe.' Lady Salisbury later replaced the hangings adding cream drapes overprinted with a pretty pink rosebud pattern which lasted until quite recently. A discreet commode placed at the side of the bed has a slide-out bottom drawer which might be used as a convenient step up to the high bed. The petite armchair was covered in a copy of a fabric that was found by Lady Beauchamp and described by her husband as 'a delightful old chintz for the furniture connected with Queen Victoria which shows her profile and that of the Prince Consort among little bunches of flowers'. The chaise longue which stood at the foot of the bed was recently reupholstered and found to have been stuffed with seaweed!

*

Lord Dalhousie, shortly after his appointment as Captain of Deal Castle, was shown over Walmer Castle by Captain Watts. Later he met the Duke by chance at Apsley House and expressed his dismay at the structural alterations thought necessary to accommodate the royal guests. 'They've knocked about your rooms a little, sir, in this royal visit,' he ventured.

The Duke agreed. Arching his eyebrows, staring at the ground and kicking out one foot before him, he muttered: 'Yes, oh yes, they have rather. Cut up Mr. Pitt's room and turned it into a dining room, but it don't signify. I'll soon knock all that down again,' he added with a knowing smile.

For it was never that easy to displace the past at Walmer.

Chapter Five

KING OF THE CASTLE

'I HAVE been painfully struck how much the Duke's sources of enjoyment and relaxation are yearly declining,' observed Stanhope in 1842. 'When I first knew him, who so fond of hunting and shooting? The latter he has for more than eight years, the former more than two relinquished. Riding he still uses as a means of health, but seems much less to delight in. . . Country visits were once very agreeable to him, from them he now wholly abstains. But what strikes me most of late is the loss of his taste for music. Formerly whenever Lady Mahon or any other lady accomplished in music dined with him, he was always eager for some songs; now he often omits to ask for or if he does ask for seems more apathetic in hearing them. . . Thus one by one all his pleasures have dropped away like leaves from a tree in winter. Only one remains – public or private business – which he transacts with undiminished alacrity.'

Wellington's gradual retreat from the social scene allowed him more time for personal leisure. He still had his duties to perform as Lord Warden and these were certainly taxing. Yet he was happiest when at Walmer. Here he could be surrounded by his friends and live out his fantasies as 'King of the Castle'. 'It is,' he once boasted, 'the most charming marine residence. The Queen herself has nothing to compare with it.'

*

The Lord Warden was responsible for appointing the captains of the 'Three Castles that Keep the Downs' – Walmer, Deal and Sandown. (It might be remembered that Deal Castle actually stands nineteen-twentieths in Walmer parish for the boundary line is marked inside the castle.) When Lord Carrington had died in office in 1838, the Duke chose his elder brother, William Wellesley-Pole, Lord Maryborough and later third Earl of Mornington, to succeed as Captain of Deal Castle.

The Duke wrote to Captain Watts giving him precise instructions to take possession of Deal Castle in the name of the Lord Warden and to direct 'Lord Carrington's servants to take great care of his property; and to seal up all that is

89

The Duke of Wellington, Lord Warden of the Cinque Ports

under lock and key, and liable to be opened.' Further, Captain Watts was to direct the porter to keep the gates shut until suitable arrangements had been made for the sale of Lord Carrington's property by auction.

When the Duke's brother also died in office, Wellington appointed the Earl – and subsequently Marquis – of Dalhousie. (His father had commanded a division in the Peninsular War and he, himself, later gained distinction as Governor-General of India.) Lord Dalhousie declared that his great delight in receiving office was primarily that it was the 'gift and goodwill from the foremost man in all the world'. Lord Dalhousie noted in his diary: (27 January 1842):

Went down to commence the arrangement of the transfer of furniture at Deal Castle. The railroad carried me as far as Ashford and a coach brought me from there to Dover by 4 o'clock. The country over which we passed latterly seemed the most hopelessly impracticable an one for railways that ever I saw, but they expect to have it into the town of Dover next year. They are working all night by torchlight, they are tunnelling through Shakespeare Cliff. . .

The Castle is a fortress built in the days of Henry VIII, having six bastions with a round tower in the centre – the whole surrounded by a dry ditch. Along the face of the tower towards the sea, Lord Carrington, the last Captain but one, built a long edifice in which are several good rooms, and very much improved the whole thing as a residence. There is an excellent drawing-room, and a great number of bedrooms of one kind or another; they are in all sorts of odd places, and of all kinds of queer shapes, but very dry and comfortable. Below there is excellent accommodation for servants of every description. The ditch is in grass with a walk round it and beautiful fruit trees trained round the circle on the walls; a good stable and a good plain kitchen garden with good fruit trees, and, thank my stars! no hot-houses or greenhouses, complete the domain.

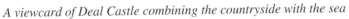

A viewcard of Deal Castle combining the countryside with the sea

The friendship between the Duke and Lord Dalhousie, which had begun so well, ended in bitter dispute. It seems Arbuthnot conspired to have Lord Dalhousie extricated from Deal Castle in favour of Lord Clanwilliam . . . and the Duke was caught in the crossfire. For once, he does not appear in a favourable light, behaving amicably to Dalhousie in public yet privately snubbing him.

Lord Dalhousie was appointed Lord Warden, with Queen Victoria's personal approval, after Wellington's death. He had, in any case, remained friendly with Captain Watts at Walmer Castle. A surviving letter demonstrates Dalhousie's magnanimity towards the Duke who does seem to have regretted the quarrel:

> The Duke's death came upon me more heavily than I could have believed. Although he did, under the intrigues of old Gosh, cast me out of Deal Castle and grew cool for shame of what he had done – for I know he said afterwards that he wished Deal Castle had been at the bottom of the sea – I loved the old man and retained real pride and gratitude in my mind for the confidence and friendship he long showed, and which I am certain he would have cordially continued to me in public to the end.

*

Edward Darby, Mayor of Deal (1842-3) who had organised many of the local celebrations during Queen Victoria's visit, was invited to dine at Walmer Castle. As he also happened to be chief magistrate at that time he was quite able to hold his own among a distinguished gathering. The Duke was most attentive towards his special guest at dinner, directing the conversation chiefly towards him. Several pertinent questions were put to the Mayor concerning the neighbourhood – and in particular the famous Deal boatmen. The Duke asked the Mayor to account for their decline in trade in recent years. He was informed that the cessation of war, the introduction of chain cables and the advent of steam tugs in the English Channel all lessened the demand for their services. The Duke listened sympathetically and then enquired tactlessly whether some of the boatmen might turn their attention to other modes of employment.

The Duke was at that time engaged in a grand project – and one which would lead directly to the decline of Deal as a port – the expansion of Dover Harbour. As chairman of the Harbour Commissioners, a post he held as Lord Warden of the Cinque Ports, the Duke was responsible for improvements and repairs to the harbour. In 1842, the enlargement of the site, which involved the excavation of five acres of land then covered with buildings, was commenced. Work was so far advanced for the Duke to attend the opening of an iron swing bridge to carry vehicles on 13 November 1846. The Duke was the first person to cross this bridge and, as he drove over in his phaeton, guns from the Redoubt fired a salute. The construction was officially named 'Wellington Bridge'.

*'The Light for All Nations' constructed on the Goodwin Sands
by William Bush in 1842*

*

The Duke kept an ever-watchful eye on the coast of France believing that a nation which had once been our enemy might be so again. He considered that the advent of steam would have a devastating effect on naval warfare and that defences along the coast should be strengthened. In 1843 he laid before Parliament a plan to fortify the Goodwin Sands as a measure to protect the English Channel but his idea was never even discussed let alone acted upon!

He was still pondering on this particular bee in his bonnet as he walked Lord Dalhousie about the castle ramparts several years later laying before the Captain his plans for building forts on Goodwin Sands to protect the Downs. 'Not a French cat,' he affirmed, 'could make its way in.'

*

The Duke was so intrigued by another scheme – to erect a fortified lighthouse on Goodwin Sands – that he helped finance the project. William Bush, a Deptford engineer, first mooted his plan to build a beacon at an estimated cost of £100,000 in 1836 and at first Trinity House gave its approval.

Bush proposed building a massive lighthouse in three sections – the lower portion consisting of a caisson to be sunk to a depth of 64 ft and then filled with a mixture of cement and shingle. Bolted to the top of this caisson would be an 86 ft tall cast-iron column with two galleries and an internal spiral staircase leading to a 40 ft lantern. The structure was to be surmounted by a patriotic statue of Queen Victoria (later changed to Britannia) and it was to be called 'The Light For All Nations'.

The Duke of Wellington was closely involved with the initial stages of the development of Bush's lighthouse. A huge base had been built at Thorncliffe Ironworks near Rotherham in Yorkshire and shipped in sections for assembly at the Navy Yard in Deal. The Duke, Lord Maryborough and a large party of interested gentlemen gathered on the beach on 18 September 1841 to watch an experiment to sink the caisson on the seabed near the old wooden pier north of the Royal Hotel. So far, so good. . .

The following month this same device was towed out to the Goodwin Sands by the steam-tug, *Monkey*. Unfortunately it ran aground and the caisson had to be cast adrift. It was washed ashore on the beach near Sandown Castle. Another steamer, *Shearwater*, rescued it and towed it back to Deal where it promptly sank.

Wrecks on the Goodwin Sands

In 1842 the caisson was salvaged, dismantled and rebuilt . . . and was once more floated out to the sands. Upon arrival at its appointed location on the North Caliper, the caisson was positioned and – despite leaning slightly and sinking alarmingly - the designer expressed complete satisfaction. Indeed, this structure survived a succession of autumn gales before being struck by an American timber ship, *Nancy*, and overturned.

Undaunted, Mr Bush made a second attempt . . . and then a third. Gradually, a modified version of his lighthouse began to take shape. By January 1845 it was sufficiently advanced for the designer and his guests to partake of a meal of roast beef and plum pudding in the partly completed living quarters and by July it was so close to completion that Bush and his family slept several nights in the chamber beneath the lantern room.

When it was finally completed, Trinity House pronounced that the lighthouse was completely impractical and dangerously situated where it would lure vessels on to the Goodwins. Mr Bush, who had invested his fortune in the project, was ordered to dismantle the entire structure. How much the Duke of Wellington had sunk into this ludicrous venture was never disclosed.

*

We have Carlyle's description of the Iron Duke at this period:

Truly a beautiful old man. I have never seen till now how beautiful and what an impression of graceful simplicity, veracity and nobleness there is about the old hero when you see him close at hand. His very size has hitherto deceived me; he is a slight, shortish figure, about five feet eight, of good breadth however, and all muscle and bone. His legs, I think, must be the short part of him, for certainly, on horseback at least, I have always taken him to be tall. Eyes, beautiful light blue, full of mild valour, with infinitely more faculty and geniality, wise, valiant and venerable.

*

Queen Victoria was in the Downs in the autumn of 1843. Her Majesty was sailing in the magnificent new twin-masted paddle steamer, *Victoria and Albert* to visit King Louis Philippe and Queen Marie Amélie at the Chateau d'Eu, near Tréport, in Normandy. This was a truly historic occasion: it was the first state visit she had paid in the new royal steam yacht, it was the first time she had visited Europe and it was further the first official visit of a British sovereign to France since Henry VIII met Francis I at the Field of Cloth of Gold in 1520. The Queen must have felt elated as she was rowed ashore in the state barge originally built for Napoleon.

A week later the Queen extended her cruise to Ostend where she was to stay with King Leopold, uncle to both Victoria and Albert. The sight of the flotilla as it once more entered the Downs was quite spectacular. The Duke described the scene to his niece, Lady Westmorland:

'Her Majesty had with her a squadron of men-at-war, three three-deckers, a 74 and others, and numerous steam vessels. The view from hence was magnificent. The day was one of the finest of the season [25 September 1843].'

Each time the royal yacht entered home waters the Duke had gone aboard to pay his respects to Her Majesty. His loyal visits were not without discomfort, however, for the Duke revealed to Lady Wilton (13 September):

The Queen made Her appearance yesterday off the South Foreland, more than two hours before Her time. However, all was ready for Her reception, the Country and Beach appearing alive [by] such Numbers of people in movement and congregating upon the latter; and the Downs by such Numbers of Boats; vessels of all sorts and sizes, navigated and propelled in every manner and going in all Directions. I rode to the Pier, where I got into a Boat and went aboard the *Ariel* steam packet which was waiting for me to step from one to the other, which had been intended; and I was obliged to get into the Boat again, and from thence into the Royal Yacht. I was most graciously received. Her Majesty and the Prince appear delighted with the Performance of their Yacht, its comforts, etc. Its speed surpasses that of everything which has appeared afloat, particularly a favourite French screw steamer of which Prince de Joinville boasted greatly.

Queen Victoria

I remained on board the Yacht for three, indeed, I believe four Hours. I did not land till seven in the evening. The wind had been from N.E. all day and there was a good deal of sea in the Downs, and the *Ariel* steamer could not be brought near enough to the Royal Yacht to enable me to walk from the latter to the former. Consequently, I was again obliged to get into the Boat, and Her Majesty saw me get a compleat Ducking on the Bottom of the ladder of the Yacht, and afterwards climb the side of the *Ariel* from the Boat.

I could not reach the Pier in the Boat from the *Ariel*. I was under the Necessity of going to the Dock Yard, where I was beached and landed after receiving as is usual in the Downs a breaker or two! However, I am not the worst for it this morning or for the trip to sea.

The Duke was quite philosophical about his ducking for he added humorously:

You will find me vastly improved since I saw you, having become in that short space of time not only a traveller by Rail Road but a Yachter. It is never too late to learn.

*

When Prime Minister, the Duke travelled from Walmer to be present at the inauguration of the first passenger train service between Liverpool and Manchester on 15 September 1830. There he witnessed the horrific accident

The Duke of Wellington's private railway carriage
(The Science Museum/Science and Society Picture Library)

where an acquaintance, William Huskisson, MP, fell on the track and was crushed. From that moment onwards the Duke had a great dislike of trains while reluctantly relying on them for his frequent visits to the capital.

In the early days of railways his journey was a tortuous one across Kent. At first he travelled by coach to Canterbury where his personal carriage – a first and second class composite built in 1838 – conveyed him on 'the Crab and Winkle Line' to Whitstable. Thence he went by boat along the Thames to London.

The designer of the Duke's carriage had taken into account the fact that he was 'a man of lofty and stately port'. Cunningly, he had concocted a deep well inside to allow for greater headroom and therefore saved the great man from bumping his head. This carriage was preserved for a time as a relic but it is now lost.

Deal acquired a station in 1847; Walmer not until 1881. After 1844 the Duke took advantage of the fast train from Dover Town Station via Ashford and Tonbridge to London Bridge. His carriage was transferred to that line and, in a compliment to their illustrious commuter, the South-Eastern Railway adopted the Duke's livery – 'Wellington brown' (a peculiar shade between terracotta and Venetian red) for their rolling stock during his lifetime.

Despite his aversion to locomotives, the Duke was passionately interested in civil engineering. The route of the South-Eastern Railway passed through Shakespeare Cliff and the three-quarters-mile tunnel, entered via gothic arches, was completed by 1843. Surprisingly, before the track was laid, the Duke walked through the entire length of the tunnel with the Marchioness of Douro and Lady Wilton, one on each arm. The dark adventure proved too much for the ladies but Wellington, unabashed, sent for his carriage. This was dragged along the shore and into the tunnel by workmen so that he and his companions could travel back in style!

The improved service from Dover took just over three hours although it still involved the Duke driving over in the early hours of the morning. He commented wryly: 'It is quite delightful to pass one's days on a Rail Road which is my common practice, and to be under the necessity of dressing every morning by candlelight in order to be in time for the trains!'

The Duke fussed over females journeying alone by railroad and resolutely avoided travelling himself on a Sunday. Even worse he was a stickler for punctuality and prided himself on never being late for a train. Once, though, he ran it very close and arrived at the station after the proper time of departure of the express from Dover. The train had actually started but as several passengers had also been left behind a second 'special' was being despatched just as the Duke arrived on the platform. 'Ha!' he cried, delighted. 'Thought I was late! Never late in my life, before. My watch must be wrong. Let it be taken to be regulated.'

All his life the Duke thought highly of the value of time. In later years he was accustomed to carrying deep in his pocket a handsome gold watch presented to him by King Ferdinand of Spain. This timepiece was a Breguet 'montres de touche' on which the hours were indicated by projecting studs round the rim of the case which enabled the owner to decipher the time by surreptitiously feeling the dial. In Victorian times it was considered extremely rude to consult a watch openly in company.

*

George Robert Gleig (1796–1888), appointed chaplain-general to the forces in 1844 and inspector-general of military schools in 1846, became vicar of Ash near Sandwich. The Duke of Wellington valued his services as an intermediary with the press and he respected his advice as an informed neighbour. Gleig is an important source for the Duke's tenancy of Walmer Castle although he claimed an intimacy with the Duke which probably never existed. Through Gleig we are able to reconstruct a typical day during the Duke's residence:

> The Duke rose at 6 o'clock every morning and, after a walk on the 'platform', read or wrote until 10 o'clock when he joined his party for breakfast. He might linger with the company, particularly if there were ladies present, or return to his study.

The drawbridge was the only entrance to Walmer Castle
in the lifetime of the Duke of Wellington

Luncheon was at 2 o'clock (although the Duke ate only twice a day: breakfast and dinner). In the afternoon he entertained his friends: he told anecdotes, rode or drove with them into the country.

At 7 o'clock he dined. Normally he dressed for dinner in the uniform of Lord Warden of the Cinque Ports – a blue coat, with scarlet collar and cuffs, and blue trousers, with a red stripe down the seam. Although he ate sparingly he kept a French chef but on state occasions he brought down a chef from London. When the menu for the day was presented to him he invariably chose a plain joint and a pudding or tart for himself. He never drank much wine and in later years abstained altogether. Yet his hospitality at table was generous.

About 9 o'clock he would say, 'Will anybody have any more wine?' and then rise and propose to go to the drawing room for coffee. It was a peculiarity of his that he always led the way, the ladies having preceded the gentlemen. In the drawing room he usually sat in an armchair near the fireplace and chatted with those of his guests that drew near him. Cards were not introduced at Walmer, but books and newspapers lay on all tables and conversation rarely flagged.

About 11 o'clock the ladies retired and half-an-hour later the Duke would say, 'I am going to bed. Whoever leaves the room last will ring for lights to be put out.' Newcomers were escorted to their bedrooms by the Duke no matter their age or rank. The little room next to his own was generally occupied by Arbuthnot or by his secretary, Algernon ('Algy') Greville. After Arbuthnot's death, the Duke's own valet slept in it.

*

The Duke was a familiar figure driving about the lanes of Walmer often attended by a single groom. He drove several vehicles: a curricle, a pair-horse phaeton or, when his house was full of guests, a type of charabanc. Being deaf, he always sat on the left hand seat in order that he might hear his companion speak.

When it rained he wore an odd assortment of cloaks and mufflers and held an umbrella over his head. He often drove long distances on shopping expeditions: to Ramsgate where he bought a red spotted handkerchief for one shilling from a draper or Dover where he ordered fifty yards of flannel from a haberdasher. During these frantic dashes about the countryside the Duke greeted passers-by with a friendly salute – two fingers to his hat – and whenever he came across any poor man who claimed to have served under him he invariably handed over a sovereign.

The Duke's driving was fast and furious and one gains the distinct impression that the roads of Walmer would have been much safer without him! Gleig relates a characteristic story:

On one occasion, I, being in the other carriage behind him, endeavoured to follow close through the narrow uneven lanes which connect Barfreston with Walmer. It was a vain effort; he was soon out of sight. Arriving by and by at the castle gate, I was met by Lord Clanwilliam, who had been the Duke's companion in the curricle. 'The Duke gets along,' was the remark. 'He soon left me behind.' 'There is no doubt of that,' was the answer, 'I thought more than once that he would have left me behind too.'

Like his driving, his horsemanship was erratic. 'The Duke rode good and safe horses,' says Lord Ellesmere, 'and I have seen him take good fences when needful.' But, according to a reporter in the *New Sporting Magazine*, his seat was 'unsightly in the extreme' and Gleig was inclined to agree that he was 'neither skilful in equitation nor an expert whip'. In truth, he was not only an indifferent judge of horses at the outset but he became so attached to an animal after he had ridden it for a time that he refused to ditch it despite its age or defects.

Consequently, the Duke had many alarming falls. To be fair he was probably not responsible for the accident which he related to Lady Salisbury when his carriage was upset upon returning from Dover. 'I was not at all hurt or put to inconvenience, except the delay of getting up again the carriage and horses.' At the time of writing he was turned eighty yet his chief concern was that the incident was not reported in the newspapers!

The Duke hunted frequently and a pack of hounds was kept in the neighbourhood for this purpose. He would willingly mount any lady or gentleman who, not having brought any horses with them, desired to watch the sport. 'The whole country is open and people can gallop away in all directions,' he affirmed to Lady Salisbury. And to Miss Burdett-Coutts: 'I am always on the Gallop.'

Occasionally the Duke attended a stag hunt at Waldershare Park, Lord Guilford's seat, or with his former antagonist, Lord Winchilsea, at Eastwell Park. 'Great heartiness' was always shown by the other gentlemen on horseback to welcome the Duke. 'Nothing the people of this county like so much as to see their great men take part in their amusements,' commented the Duke. 'The aristocracy will commit a great error if they ever fail to mix freely with their neighbours.' At such times the Duke cut a gay figure: 'a scarlet frockcoat, a lilac silk waistcoat, kid gloves, and a pair of fustian trousers strapped tightly down over a pair of Wellington boots' was one contemporary description of his hunting attire.

A curious incident concerning hunting occurred long after the Duke had died. In the spring of 1889 the West Street Harriers, following a hare across the countryside near St Margaret's Bay, lost the hare but started a fox. There was a dramatic chase across Kingsdown Cliffs and into Lower Walmer where the fox was diverted because of a football match at Marke Wood into the castle grounds. Thereupon it made for the safety of the moat and after a rapid circuit dashed across the drawbridge and into the castle itself. Here the hounds pursued their quarry. Earl Granville, the present Lord Warden, was alerted by the commotion and was just in time to see the fox killed by the pack in the corridor immediately outside the Duke's Room.

*

We are fortunate to have yet another impression of Wellington at Walmer about this time from the diarist, Thomas Raikes. This wealthy dandy and frequenter of clubs venerated the Duke more as a Tory statesman than as a soldier.

Saturday 23 September 1843: I went down to Walmer Castle, and found the Duke with Mr Arbuthnot on the rampart, or, as it is called, the platform, which overlooks the sea. Some officers belonging to the ships in the Downs came to dinner. . . The conversation of the Duke was, as usual, interesting on every subject, his memory surprising, and his knowledge of naval matters and naval architecture as great as if it were his own province.

Monday 9 October: The Duke is certainly growing old and feeble, which, though much to be regretted, is not surprising, but he never will allow anyone to do anything for him. Greville says: 'If he drops his hat I should never think of stooping to pick it up – he would not like it.' He will get up himself to ring the bell; and I observe at night, when we retire to bed, he will light your flat candlestick and give it to you. His politeness is unceasing to all; and here in his own house it is only to be equalled by his kindness and cordiality.

He rises very early; perhaps does not give himself time for sleep. He is always a very long time dressing, as he shaves himself, though his hand is unsteady, and never will allow a servant to assist him.

Wednesday 11 October: We left Walmer, having fixed tomorrow for our return. As every memorial will be interesting hereafter of the habits and characteristics of one whose name will fill the pages of history, I shall add a few details of the Duke's daily life at Walmer. He always rises at six o'clock, and walks on the platform, then returns to his room to dress, which, as I have said, takes a very long time. He is remarkably neat in his appearance always wearing a white waistcoat and trowsers, under which is a good guard of fleecy hosiery against the cold; and a blue riding coat in the morning.

At ten o'clock he appears at breakfast, and makes messes of rusks and bread in his tea, never meat or eggs. He converses the whole time, then retires, saying, 'Well we shall dine at seven.' He remains in his room, writing letters and despatches, and making notes, some rather droll and concise, on the different letters to be answered by his secretary in his name; and Greville's hand is become so like to his, that few people can distinguish the difference. . .

102

About two o'clock he generally gets on his horse, and gallops over the downs, or, perhaps, to Dover, where he is very active in attending to his business as Warden of the Cinque Ports. He seems to be worshipped all over the country, for he is very charitable and always ready to do good to his neighbours. . .

On his return he walks again on the platform, till he enters to dress for dinner, at which he also eats with appetite, mixing meat, rice and vegetables into a mess, which fills his plate; he drinks very little wine, and

Victorian pot lid depicting the Duke riding near Walmer Castle

during the evening, two decanters of iced water are placed at his side, which are generally empty when he goes to bed.

When we are only men, he dressed in boots, but when there are ladies (and when only my daughter) always wears shoes, silk stockings, with his star and garter. He is exceedingly polite to all, and particularly attentive to women.

Although still active, yet age has made some havoc with his frame; his hair is quite white, but not scanty; he is very deaf with the left ear, and when left to himself or engaged in thought, he stoops very much, and his head seems to droop on his breast, but the instant any subject is started that interests him, his eye brightens, his head is raised, he puts his hand to his right ear to catch the sound, and enters into the argument with all the spirit, and judgement, and penetration, which form so striking a part of his character.

*

In August 1847, Francis William Fane, Lord Westmorland's third son, who was then a young subaltern in the 74th Regiment, was staying at Walmer Castle while recovering from an attack of fever. He was entirely alone with the Duke and Charles Arbuthnot, and regretted in later life not having made notes of their reminiscences.

One evening the Duke surprised him by suddenly asking: 'Francis, do you mind hot weather?'

'No, sir.'

'Are you fond of drink?'

'No, sir. I don't like wine.'

'Oh, very well. . .' And here the matter seemed to end but that night the Duke wrote to his niece, Lady Westmorland, offering to recommend her son for India. In due course, Francis Fane was appointed Aide-de-Camp to Lord Dalhousie, Governor General of India.

Indeed, young Fane must have greatly impressed the Duke who rarely procured favours for his friends or relatives.

*

Old St Mary's Church at Walmer

Whenever a senior officer proposed to inspect troops stationed at Dover Castle or Walmer Barracks, the Duke was notified and, as a rule, attended in his official role of the Lord Warden. Gleig relates the time when the depots of two regiments were formed into one small battalion at Walmer and the Duke was duly invited to attend the inspection. The Duke watched as the major put his troops through their paces and then obliged him to place his battalion in line between the spire of a chapel and a windmill standing in fields southwards of the parade ground. (This feat can only be accomplished, apparently, by two men or more mutually dressing each other on the points respectively.) Gleefully, the Duke watched the major struggling with this problem for some time before he good humouredly demonstrated how it could be done. Afterwards, in the course of his ride homewards, the Duke set to work on the Downs drilling his party of friends who had witnessed this complicated military exercise.

*

Opening the gate for the Duke at Walmer Church (St Mary's Church, Walmer)

The Duke of Wellington was a regular worshipper at the ancient parish church of Saint Mary at Upper Walmer. Every Sunday, without fail, he rode over from the castle, a great Bible tucked under his arm, and tied up his horse to the yew tree near the porch. The Duke's pew was a large old-fashioned square one that stood almost immediately under the triple-decker pulpit with its quaint sounding

The Duke of Wellington in his private pew at Old St Mary's Church
(St Mary's Church Walmer)

board affixed to the wall above the heavily-draped plain windows of the south aisle. It was situated in the annexe on the north side, since demolished.

Gleig mentions that the Duke received the sacrament as often as it was administered. 'It was a touching sight to see that great and venerable man, kneeling devotedly before the altar rails of the village church, with the sunlight falling through the stained glass upon his head, and his own attention fixed entirely upon the act in which he was participating.'

He was not always so attentive during the sermon for, unless the preacher was eloquent, or the subject out of the ordinary, he used to gather himself up into one corner of his pew and fall asleep, snoring loudly.

The Duke was most particular that his guests should attend divine service. Count Nugent, an Austrian general who hailed originally from Ireland, paid him a visit at Walmer Castle. When the time came to go to church the Count declined, explaining he was a Catholic.

'Oh, very well,' was the answer and, turning to Captain Watts, who happened to be in the same room, the Duke pointedly enquired:

'Count Nugent wants to go to the Roman Catholic Chapel. Do you know where it is?'

Captain Watts replied in the affirmative.

'Then be so good as to show him the way.' There was no point in the Count protesting further: to the Catholic Church he went!

The Duke was a great deal tickled by this incident and in walking to church with his Protestant companions observed: 'I know he did not want me to go to church, nor to go himself either, but I thought it best we should both go.'

One Sunday morning a certain pew was occupied by some ladies who were visitors to the village. They had been ushered there upon entering the church by the churchwarden who had concluded that, since he was late, the usual occupier had no intention of attending that morning. Presently this good parishioner appeared and, without any hesitation, turned the whole party out into the aisle. There they stood, all eyes gazing upon them, deeply confused and acutely embarrassed. Promptly, the Duke of Wellington rose from his seat, opened the door of his own private pew and politely invited them inside.

Another Sunday morning, shortly before the Duke's death, a young artist set up her palette in the meadow on the seaward side of Walmer Castle. As she was making her preliminary sketch, the Duke himself appeared on his way to divine service. Noticing her, he crossed the meadow and peered over her shoulder to see how her drawing was progressing. 'Very like, very like,' he observed and, smiling, he continued on his way. The artist recorded this amusing incident by adding the Duke to one corner of her picture which was later turned into a popular engraving. The Duke appears wearing his distinctive top hat passing through the kissing gate which still exists in the castle paddock.

*

The Duke so much admired the young artist's sketch of Walmer Castle when he stopped to inspect it on his way to church that she added his figure to her finished painting –far right (St Mary's Church, Walmer)

The Duke was an indefatigable letter writer – averaging fifty letters a day – though sometimes the nature of his correspondence was trivial. Occasionally, he communicated in French since he had a good command of that language. All kinds of people wrote to him and he answered indiscriminately – very often to the effect that he resented being the recipient of a letter! Once, while at Walmer, he received an invitation to the wedding of a young relative in town although the bridegroom's mother – mad in his estimation! – had given the time but omitted to name the location. The unfortunate woman received a rocket blast: 'I cannot go about the streets on Thursday morning seeking for the place at which W. Wellesley is to be married to Miss Drummond.'

One of Lady Charles Wellesley's fondest memories was of catching sight of the Duke at work at his desk near the window of his study 'the sun shining on his silvery hair'. It was one of his obstinacies to refuse to wear spectacles. Consequently his writing grew almost illegible in old age. Worst still, he often wrote only parts of words or omitted them altogether! He was particularly proud of being long-sighted and used to boast that he could distinguish the flags on distant ships passing up and down the Channel without the aid of a 'sea spying glass'. He even asserted that from the castle ramparts at night he could discern the lights from the town of Calais. Certainly, on still summer evenings this would be perfectly feasible.

*

After Charles Arbuthnot's death in 1850, the Duke was quite often alone at Walmer for weeks on end. He found a new friend, however, in the young Lady Mary de la Warr who, in 1847, had become the second Lady Salisbury. The Duke had become acquainted with Mary as early as 1835 when, as a child of eleven, she had been staying with her family at Walmer. Wellington had walked with her to church and called her his 'little friend'.

The new Lady Salisbury became a frequent visitor to Walmer and the Duke was pleased to lend her his castle whenever he was absent. 'You must know Walmer Castle as well as I do, otherwise I would send you the plan. . .' They soon became regular correspondents.

One of the oddest gifts the Duke presented to her was a sample of the new submarine cable from Dover Harbour. 'It is very curious. In fact it is a rope made of brass wire half the thickness of a little finger. . .' The project fascinated him. After all, if messages could be transmitted twenty-five miles, they might just as well travel one hundred. . .

The Duke had become interested in astronomy ever since he had purchased a book on that subject at the sale of Lord Carrington's effects at Deal Castle. He kept a telescope specifically for that purpose at Walmer Castle. He laughed when Lady Salisbury discovered the book in his study, complete with all his 'marks and places', and he wondered whether she, too, might become an amateur star-gazer?

*

Launching a Deal boat in a storm

In August 1850 Queen Victoria and Prince Albert were again off Deal on their return from Holland. The royal yacht anchored in the Downs for the night and the Duke put off in a small rowing boat to pay his respects. On his return he received the inevitable soaking. According to Pritchard:

> On coming to the beach again as the flood-tide was making, a heavy swell rose up (a very common occurrence) and rolling waves pitched into the boat, which nearly swamped her. The Duke stuck fast to his seat, escaping by only having got a good sousing which apparently did not in the least discompose his wonted equanimity, for he no sooner found his foot on the beach than he mounted his horse and rode home to the castle regardless of the accident.

*

Lord Brougham invited himself to Walmer Castle in the autumn of 1850 on his route to Germany. The Duke had anticipated this visit and dreaded his coming. In October his guest arrived and the Duke artfully laid before him a timetable of all the vessels sailing from the coast the following day. . . 'Otherwise I might have had the pleasure of his company for a month.'

The following year brought further unwelcome guests: Prince Frederick of the Netherlands (son of King William II of Holland) and with him, Field-Marshal Nugent, now more mindful of his devotions. The Duke wrote on 9 October: 'I have had all my guests here since yesterday; and am heartily tired of them! I do not know when they go! I am really so deaf as to be entirely unfit for social life! But here I am obliged to sit from morning till night – in fruitless endeavour to entertain people, who have no means of entertaining themselves.'

The Duke had lost his hearing owing to a misguided doctor's primitive cure for deafness which involved injecting a strong caustic solution into his ear in 1826. In later life he suffered also from rheumatism which gave his neck the fixed stoop which sadly marred his figure.

Even in profound old age the soldier-statesman was regarded as an eligible partner by Victorian society ladies. Internationally famous, phenomenally wealthy, courteous, kind and witty . . . he was lionised throughout his life in town and country by adoring females. Secretly they secured snippets of his silvery-brown hair after his monthly haircut in order to wear with his portrait in their lockets.

His relationships with gentlewomen were notorious although, it would seem, they were conducted with strict propriety. Nevertheless, certain dalliances invited speculation, gossip, malice and even attempted blackmail . . . but at any suggestion of marriage the Duke threw back his head and roared with laughter!

The Duke's most intimate friendship in later years was with the millionairess, Miss Angela Burdett-Coutts, sole heiress to Coutts Bank. Their supposed 'romance' took place largely in London but there were frequent rendezvous at Walmer. Once, though, Miss Burdett-Coutts overstepped the boundaries of decency by arriving unannounced at the castle where she received a crushing rebuke from the Duke. To observe propriety in future, she proposed renting a house on Walmer Beach but in any case their scandalous 'affair' dwindled when she decided to tour the Continent.

The Duke held a Pilot Court at Dover in October 1850. Afterwards he went to call on the children of a new lady friend, Mrs Margaret Jones, wife of an MP, but found their lodgings in Biggin Street deserted. 'They and the Governess must have gone as all others in Dover to see the Shew,' he wrote to her later, 'at the very same time at which the Shew went to see them!'

*

In the summer of 1852 it was announced that the Queen intended a cruise to Belgium to visit Prince Leopold. The Duke hurried down to the coast, accompanied only by his valet, in order to receive Her Majesty should she decide to land on her journey from Osborne to Ostend. 'She will anchor at Dover possibly to look at the Western Heights; at all events to allow Prince Albert to see them,' he informed Lady Salisbury. 'If she should anchor in the Downs I ought to be there. However if I go it will be only for a few days.' Dutifully, on 7 August, Wellington was installed at Walmer Castle where he was formally attended by the Cinque Ports Pilots.

At 5 p.m. on 10 August the royal yacht, *Victoria and Albert*, entered the Downs. The sea proved boisterous so Her Majesty preferred to stay on board ship. Prince Albert braved the seas, however, and passed a pleasant hour with the Duke strolling in the castle grounds.

Lady Salisbury must have expected the Queen to visit him for the Duke wrote to her: 'It is curious that you were thinking of the Queen being at Walmer Castle; while I was thinking of you going on board to pay my respects to Her Majesty. It never occurred to me to be possible to starve Her Majesty upon the cookery of Mrs Allen's cuisine. I was inspired that I should be ducked again on my visit to the Queen, as I had been in the one paid two or three years ago. But I regretted that I did not go off with Prince Albert when he returned to the Yacht after visiting me at the Castle.'

In the morning the royal squadron pursued its course while the Duke drove across to Dover there to catch the train to London. When the royal couple passed through the Downs on their return journey towards the end of the month they missed seeing the Duke because he was still in town. Lost opportunities, certainly, for the Duke never again set eyes on his sovereign.

The Duke's last official visit to Dover Harbour

Chapter Six

WELLINGTON'S LAST DAYS AT WALMER

'I ARRIVED here prosperously yesterday evening and I never saw the castle looking so well,' the Duke of Wellington wrote on 27 August 1852 to Lady Salisbury who had been spending the summer at Walmer. 'The fields at the back of the beach were quite green, the sky without a cloud, the sea calm and blue; and everything in tranquillity. I did immediately what I do not doubt was the last thing you did previously to your departure. I walked on the Tower above and on the platform below. . . It is certainly a most delightful residence. I understand that the Queen came in quite close on her passage from Ostend. The Royal Standard was hoisted and a Royal Salute fired. They say that She came in so close as to be known from the platform. I conclude that She thought it probable that I had come down here. I slept in my little camp bed without curtains, which amused you so much! Indeed, I think I like it better for the notice taken of it.'

Sir Arthur Wellesley, Duke of Wellington, had arrived for the last time at Walmer Castle after 'a very good journey in less than four hours from my house in London.' He had brought with him his whole establishment of servants, horses and carriages – a sufficient indication that his autumnal sojourn had begun. It had been settled in advance that Lord and Lady Salisbury would return to the Castle in September. Meanwhile, he had promised to entertain a Russian Princess and her suite – a visit he was not relishing. 'I wish,' he despaired, 'that my Imperial Royalties were in Russia.'

Forthwith, the Duke received Her Imperial Highness the Grand Duchess Catherine of Russia and her husband, His Serene Highness Duke George of Mecklenburg-Strelitz. This was an occasion for great festivity. The Princess was attended by Baron Brunnow, the Russian minister and his private secretary; Earl of Clanwilliam, Captain of Deal Castle; Admiral Sir John Hill, Captain of Sandown Castle; Captain Vincent, RN, Captain of Sandgate Castle; and Captain Watts. The latter remarked: 'I never saw the Duke in better health or spirits.'

The Russian Princess, in the event, touched the Duke's heart – 'My little Duchess' he calls her in a letter to Lady Westmorland - and he unhooked a portrait of himself from the dining room wall and offered it to her, saying in

113

A pair of Wellington boots displayed at Walmer Castle (English Heritage)

French, 'It is the very best likeness that was ever taken of me.' He rang the bell and desired his butler to remove the picture from the frame for him to sign, which he did – first trying the pen – on the following day.

This particular portrait had been painted by a Portuguese artist after the Battle of Talavera. It was a proof engraving which the Duke – to his chagrin – later discovered was irreplaceable. Lord Ellesmere intriguingly noted that the picture was 'remarkable for the size and strength of the legs'. Underneath the engraver had inscribed the single Latin word, 'Invicto', to which the Duke had added in pencil, 'Don't cry until you are out of the wood.'

When the time came for his royal guest to depart for Ostend, the Duke drove the Princess personally in his pony carriage to Dover. They were welcomed with a royal salute from the Heights. Then, having taken leave of her at the Ship Hotel, the Duke, as Lord Warden, inspected the works still in progress at Dover Harbour. He took an invigorating stroll along the partly constructed Admiralty Pier in the company of Mr Iron, the harbourmaster.

This was his last official visit. The Duke was now quite alone with his domestics at Walmer Castle.

*

On Wednesday 1st September the Duke travelled by train to see his friends, the Salisburys, at Buckhurst Park near Tunbridge Wells. The following day he had a disastrous expedition to Folkestone. He had intended visiting his old friend, John Wilson Croker, an invalid who had moved there in search of health. After riding over to Dover the Duke took a train to Folkestone where he was informed that Radnor Place was nearby. No fly being available, he set out resolutely to walk and discovered that Croker's house was a good three miles across the valley . . . 'through the town, down hill, then up a steep hill'. At the end of his

114

trek he was told that Croker had gone to Dover – where the Duke met him on his march back!

Two days later the Duke set out once more unaccompanied to Folkestone and when they finally met the two friends spent a pleasant few hours reminiscing about old times. 'The Duke chatted in a most agreeable manner on all manner of subjects,' Croker later reported, 'with a vivacity and memory worth noting of a man in his eighty-fourth year.'

As before, the Duke had strolled over to Radnor Place without a guide and he had commented that he had found the walk quite strenuous being more hilly than he had expected. Croker laughed. 'It seems you forgot to guess what was on the other side of the hill!' (This referred to a circumstance which had occurred between the two men thirty years before. When travelling in the north they had amused themselves by guessing what sort of country lay ahead as they drove up the side of each hill. Croker had expressed surprise at the time at some extraordinarily accurate guesses Wellington had made to which the Duke replied: 'Why, I have spent all my life in trying to guess what was on the other side of the hill.')

Mrs Croker looked puzzled until the Duke explained the allusion: 'All the business of war and indeed all the business of life is to endeavour to find out what you don't know by what you do know; that's what I called guessing what was on the other side of the hill.'

And so the time slipped by. . . When The Duke's carriage arrived he walked slowly down the steps counting them aloud for his friend's guidance. At the station a tipsy Irishman sporting a Peninsular medal begged the inevitable sovereign. Then the Duke returned to Walmer.

There his generosity still prevailed. A letter arrived from a total stranger purporting to be an officer's widow stranded in Boulogne and pleading for her fare home. The Duke duly obliged with five pounds. In a few days time came another missive – the lady in her excitement at receiving the money had broken a looking glass and would His Grace provide a further five pounds? 'Was there ever anything like it in the World!'

Every morning the mail at Walmer had brought requests of a similar nature to which the Duke answered indiscriminately. Once Arbuthnot entered the Duke's room to find him stuffing bank notes into several envelopes. 'What are you doing, Duke?' he enquired.

'Doing? Doing what I am obliged to do every day. It would take the wealth of the Indies to meet all the demands that are made upon me.'

Lord and Lady Charles Wellesley arrived at the castle with their children which greatly delighted the Duke. He spent an enjoyable few days with his grandchildren making them companions in his strolls about the grounds or backwards and forwards along the path which ran between the castle and the sea.

On the Saturday he rode over unannounced to Dover to inspect the harbour works; on the Sunday he went as usual to Walmer Church where the congregation noticed he looked a little pale. An unremarkable weekend . . . except for one small incident. While he was writing in his study, a letter was handed to him which had just that moment been delivered to the castle. It purported to be from 'a messenger from the Lord' who would call and deliver his missive in person on the following morning. The Duke was sceptical: 'We shall see . . .'

*

On Monday 13 September, the Duke rose at 5.30 to look at his garden. He remained in high spirits throughout that day. He visited the stables and gave instructions to the groom to send his carriage to Dover on the morrow to collect Lady Westmorland who was to join the house party. He wrote to Lady Salisbury making arrangements for her to visit him on the following Wednesday. 'God bless you my dear, with my constant wishes for your children, believe me as ever. . .' he ended his letter. Then, peering out of his window, he added a postcript: 'The wind has changed to the West, but it is cold.'

Braving the cold, he rode out to view the coastline and inspect the defences. Then he played with his grandchildren. In the evening he ate heartily: mock turtle soup, turbot and venison. Around 8.30 p.m. he retired, carrying his saveall with flickering candle down the long, dark passage, to his study where he read in bed.

The wind had changed. It had been his last full day.

*

Kendall, his valet, knocked on his door at six o'clock in the morning of 14 September to wake him. The Duke appeared to be sleeping heavily. He must have felt cold in the night for he had drawn his military cloak over his shoulders. The old retainer banked up the fire mindful not to disturb his master.

Soon after one of the maids met him and said she was afraid the Duke was ill for she had heard him groan. Kendall returned at once, pulled back the shutters and announced: 'It is getting quite late, Your Grace. It is past seven o'clock.'

'Is it?' replied the Duke in his usual tone of voice. 'Do you know where the apothecary lives?'

'Yes, your Grace.'

'Then send for him and let him know that I should like to see him. I don't feel quite well and I will lie still till he comes.'

This was an extraordinary admission for the Duke. A messenger was dispatched immediately on horseback for Mr Hulke's house, 'Comarques', in the High Street at Deal. The apothecary left his breakfast unfinished and reached the castle at nine o'clock. 'I am sorry that Your Grace is an invalid – what do

116

you complain of?' Mr Hulke enquired solicitously.

'I think some derangement,' he replied indicating his chest.

After his examination Mr Hulke pronounced that the Duke was merely suffering from acute indigestion. Finding no cause for alarm, Mr Hulke ordered tea and toast to be followed by an ammonia stimulant. After promising Lord Charles that he would return at noon, the apothecary departed.

As soon as he had gone, Kendall asked the Duke if he would take some tea.

'Yes, if you please.'

Simple words, but they underline the Duke's politeness even in the face of illness. And they were the last he spoke. Tea was followed by a series of violent fits until the Duke slipped into unconsciousness.

*

By this time the whole household was disturbed. Lord and Lady Charles Wellesley crept into the bedroom followed by Captain Watts. Again they summoned Mr Hulke who came with his son and Dr MacArthur. These three doctors administered their various primitive remedies – they gave the Duke a

A contemporary engraving showing the death scene. The Duke is surrounded by his family, doctors and servants

The room where the Duke died became a shrine in Victorian times

strong emetic, applied mustard poultices and irritated his jaws with a feather – but all to no effect. It soon became apparent that the Duke's last hour had come.

His anxious attendants, perceiving that he breathed with difficulty, lifted the Duke into his high chair taking care to wrap his legs in a blanket and placing a cushion between his knees. Nothing was achieved by this change of position. Violent fits increased until at last the Duke ceased to breathe. The time was 3.25 p.m.

At first the Duke's family did not realise that he had passed away until Kendall held a mirror to his mouth. The polished surface remained undimmed.

The Messenger of the Lord had come for him. . .

*

Priscilla, Lady Westmorland, the Duke's favourite niece, was expected that day at the castle. She had arrived at Dover Town Station a little surprised that the Duke was not there to greet her. Earlier that morning she had received at her London address a letter from him appointing to meet her at Dover. Idly, she had given the note to the small boy of the friends with whom she was staying and allowed him to tear it up into tiny pieces and scatter it playfully over the carpet. Little did she think at the time of the importance which might be attached to this – the Duke's last letter.

Eventually, Lord Clanwilliam arrived with a note from Lord Charles Wellesley saying that the Duke was too ill to travel. Clanwilliam hinted that matters were serious. Directly, Lady Westmorland ordered a fly to take her to Walmer where she was greatly dismayed to find Townsend, head gardener, waiting for her at the gate. Tearfully he related the sad news: 'It's all over – he is gone.'

Charles Dickens was walking in Walmer that same afternoon unaware that the Iron Duke had died. When he returned to his lodgings at Dover that evening he received the sorry news and wrote forthwith to his friend, Angela Burdett-Coutts:

10 Camden Crescent,
Dover.

14 September 1852

My Dear Miss Coutts,

I have just heard of what you will have long been prepared for, but what I fear will cause you, notwithstanding, some natural distress. I was walking at Walmer this afternoon, and little thought that the great old man was dying or dead. He had been a steady friend of an uncle of Mrs Dickens who was Colonel of Engineers here; and his son left word, a little while ago, while we were at dinner, that the Duke was dead.

Ever, Dear Miss Coutts,
Most Faithfully Yours,
Charles Dickens.

*

Immediately, the town of Deal went into mourning: it mirrored the mood of the nation. All the shops were closed, the streets were deserted and flags flew at half-mast. Even the weather added to the air of sorrow. Despondency prevailed. The body of the Duke lay quietly at first on his camp bed awaiting the embalmers. Then the weird business of requesting souvenirs began which epitomises the Victorian attitude to death. The Duke's walrus ivory false teeth were removed and presented to Lady Douro; a marble replica of the Duke's hands was commissioned by Miss Coutts while endless snippets of hair were despatched to relatives and friends. Even Mr Hulke pocketed a pair of shoe buckles!

*

Three days later the Duke's death mask was cast. The sculptor and medallist, George Gammon Adams (1821-1898) received this important commission. *The*

119

Death mask of the Duke (Sotheby's)

Times reported (18 September 1852) that Mr Adams '. . . has been fortunate enough to secure a Cast of the Duke's face, and this memorial of him will, no doubt, hereafter be highly valued as an authentic likeness.'

From this cast Adams produced a bust which, according to *The Times*, was so perfect a likeness that orders for it had been received 'from the Queen, the present Duke, Lord Hardinge, the Duke of Buccleuch, the Marquis of Teeddale, the Earl of Ellesmere, and a large number of the personal 'friends of the illustrious deceased.' It was from this bust that a funeral medal was cast.

The original cast of the death mask, still with impressions of threads and traces of the original mould, was retained by Adams. At the end of his life his young wife gave birth to a daughter, Ivy Dorothea, who lived on, as the sole representative of the family, until 1984. Miss Adams' effects, the mask included, were bequeathed to her housekeeper. Recently the mask came up for auction at Sotheby's and was acquired for the Wellington Museum at Apsley House.

A later, dark-brown, electro-type made from this mask was presented by the second Duke to the Royal Institution. Yet another version is preserved at Walmer Castle.

The original mask was made from plaster and extended to the ear only on the right side. Death masks are an anathema to modern eyes but before the advent of photography they captured the exact likeness – albeit in death – of the most celebrated figures in British and European history. Adams' mask is arguably the most authentic portrait of the Duke of Wellington to survive.

*

Queen Victoria requested a lock of hair. Kendal obliged and wrote to a footman at Windsor: 'Lord Douro the present Duke told me that Her Majesty was desirous for a piece of the poor Duke's hair and the last Hand laid on the body was mine to cut off a lock of Hair from the Head. . . The Coffin was instantly soldered down, the poor Duke's remains never to be seen more.' (23 September 1852).

The death certificate, signed by Mr William Hulke's son, John, 'present at the death', names the deceased as 'Arthur Wellesley / Male 83 years / Field-Marshal Duke of Wellington K.G., G.C.B., G.C.H.' and records the cause of death as 'epilepsy'.

*

Mr Hulke was besieged with letters of condolences. The Salisburys were devastated by the news of the Duke's death since they had been on the point of leaving their home, Buckhurst Park, Tunbridge Wells, to pay a return visit to their friend at Walmer Castle. Typical was Lord Salisbury's request: 'When you have a moment of leisure, a few particulars of the last moments will be most acceptable. . .'

Queen Victoria's locket containing a snippet of Wellington's hair
(His Grace the Duke of Wellington, KG, Stratfield Saye House, Hampshire)

Artists were busily capturing those 'last moments' on canvas and the sale of engraved copies to a grieving public was a lucrative business. Walmer Castle was depicted with the Union Jack at half-mast; the Duke was resurrected to appear in his study and the minutiae of mourning were artistically recorded.

And here Mr. Hulke unwittingly gave offence to the second Duke. The celebrated artist, William Henry Fisk (1827-1884), landscape painter and anatomical draughtsman, was intent upon painting the death scene of the Duke of Wellington for a summer exhibition at the Royal Academy. He considered that, if he were to achieve a 'truthful representation' in oils, then his painting was best done 'while the circumstances are most vividly impressed on the minds of those present on the occasion'. (Although this might be wise in artistic terms, it was hardly a sensitive approach to the bereaved family.)

Fisk moved swiftly. He approached Kendall to provide a thumbnail sketch of the family and medics as they had appeared in the Duke's room. Then he prevailed upon Mr Hulke – 'as chief medical attendant' – to pose for a daguerrotype so that his portrait could be incorporated by the artist into one of his historical tableaux for which he eventually became famous. The second Duke was furious. He fumed at Mr Hulke in a letter scrawled on black-edged notepaper pointing out the pain and distress such a project would naturally cause his family. Prudently, Mr Hulke withdrew. Fisk's painting was probably abandoned; it certainly did not feature in any Academy Exhibition.

Yet a popular print did appear portraying the family and friends gathered about their dying hero in a souvenir edition of *The Illustrated London News*. This was a wood engraving – the combined effort of Sir John Gilbert and Joseph L. Williams – which accurately recorded for posterity the melancholy scene.

*

The coffin surmounted by a ducal coronet

Poets also penned their tributes. These literary efforts were hastily composed to accompany stark engravings of Walmer Castle. Their mood was sombre, fanciful, patriotic, occasionally even metaphysical.

Tennyson, the new Poet Laureate, wrote a long 'Ode' beginning:

> Bury the Great Duke
> With an Empire's lamentation,
> Let us bury the Great Duke
> To the noise of mourning
> Of a mighty nation.

The American poet, Henry Longfellow (1807-82), who had greater success with *Hiawatha*, composed an atmospheric poem imagining Death, disguised as

Thousands of mourners sought entrance to the castle

an ethereal warrior, creeping through the autumn mist rolling down the English Channel, to steal away the soul of 'the old Field Marshal':

> He passed into the chamber of the sleeper,
>   The dark and silent room,
> And as he entered, darker grew and deeper,
>   The silence and the gloom.
>
> He did not pause to parley or dissemble,
>   But smote the Warden hoar;
> Ah! what a blow! that made all England tremble,
>   And groan from shore to shore.

The line of mourners stretched along Walmer beach

would stop, wait and then gently continue along the familiar road for home. And then there were the worshippers at the tiny village church who could remember with affection the most famous and devout member of their congregation well into this present century. . .

The Duke of Wellington's hatchment displayed at Walmer Church shows the single Order of the Garter

As was the custom, the Duke's hatchment (a pictorial lozenge-shaped board displaying his armorial bearings or 'achievements') was solemnly placed in Old Saint Mary's Church. There his pew, the pulpit and the reading desk would have been draped in black as a mark of respect to his memory.

Today the hatchment hangs high on the north wall directly over the site of the Duke's rented pew which stood in the annexe, since demolished. Curiously, the hatchment displays only one of his innumerable orders – the Order of the Garter. The arms are surmounted by a ducal coronet out of which appears a lion rampant holding a forked pennant charged with the cross of Saint George. In importance the Duke's orders were said at the time to have exceeded in number and importance anything of the kind ever possessed by a single individual.

*

128

---

*

For a full two months, while Parliament deliberated upon an elaborate state funeral, the Duke lay in the 'dark and silent' room where he had died. The study was draped with black velvet; giant candelabra and black plumes surrounded the coffin while candles reflecting against their silver sconces on the walls barely lifted the gloom. A guard of honour composed of a section of the Duke's Own Rifle Regiment with hands resting on arms reversed stood sentinel day and night.

The Marquis of Douro, the Duke's eldest son, chanced to be abroad at the time of his father's death and he was notified by electric telegraph. Meanwhile the remainder of the noble family gathered at the castle and on Sunday 19 October a service was read for them in the drawing room by the Revd Gerald Wellesley, the Duke's nephew.

The funeral cortège passing Deal Castle

For two days, 9 and 10 November, the inhabitants of Deal and Walmer were admitted to the castle to pay their last respects. Over 9,000 people availed themselves of this privilege. A slow solemn line of mourners dressed solely in black passed through the castle.

Then on the evening of 11 November the hearse drawn by four black plumed horses and followed by three mourning coaches left the castle watched by silent crowds. The first coach contained the second Duke and Captain Watts; the second held a representative of the Lord Chamberlain while the third carried those faithful servants, Collins and Kendall. The cortège proceeded at an exceedingly slow pace, escorted by mutes with flambeaux and attended by one

125

The hearse arrives at Deal Railway Station

hundred and fifty members of the Rifle Regiment.

Minute guns fired from the three castles – first Walmer, then Deal, last Sandown. At Deal Station the body was received by Mr James Macgregor, MP, Chairman of the South-Eastern Railway Company. Entrained, the coffin departed at a quarter past nine for London.

*

The Duke lay in state at Chelsea Hospital while preparations were finalised for the greatest state funeral that our nation had ever witnessed. Then, on 18 November, the body began its last tortuous journey for burial with full honours during a moving memorial service at St Paul's Cathedral. The spectacular procession was watched by over one million people in brilliant sunshine.

The ornate triumphal car which carried the coffin was composed of metal from guns captured at Waterloo. Its design was 'inspired' by the Prince Consort but was judged 'abominably ugly' and 'monstrously inefficient' since it proved awkward to manoeuvre. After the ceremony it was hidden for over a century in the cathedral crypt but was discovered this last decade – though not immediately recognised – and it is now on display at Stratfield Saye.

Throughout his life the Duke was often heard to say: 'Where the tree falls, there let it lie.' If Wellington's wish had been fulfilled, and the public had not laid claim to his body, he might have been buried in a humble grave in Walmer churchyard . . .

*

The people of Deal and Walmer felt that they had lost a dear friend. An old fisherman who had lived his entire life within a stone's throw of the castle thought that there had been no occupant 'quite so homely as our Duke'. A lady recalled that, as a young girl, she used to open the tollgate at Upper Deal for the Duke to pass. Often, she said, he was sound asleep in the saddle so the horse

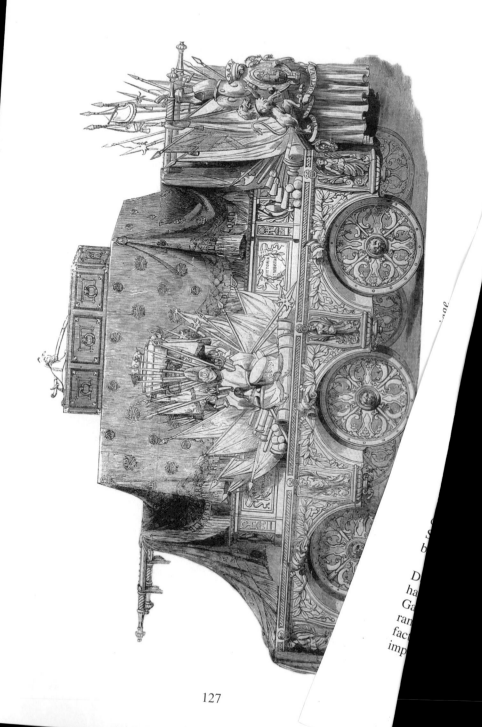

The Duke's furniture, upon his demise, became the property of his heirs. (It was the custom of the time that the furniture could be bought by the succeeding Lord Warden, if desired, and in that manner Wellington himself had acquired several fine pieces which had belonged to William Pitt.) Lord Palmerston, when appointed Lord Warden, declined to buy the Duke's furniture – which had remained in situ – and offered it at auction. Prudently, the second Duke stepped in and claimed several personal items including the camp bed, the bed table and the armchair, which were carefully stored at Apsley House.

Later, through the generosity of another Lord Warden, W. H. Smith, the remainder of the Duke's furniture was presented as heirlooms to the castle. Lady Reading, during her husband's brief tenure (1934-5) endeavoured to restore 'the Duke's Room' to its original appearance. Diligently, she consulted paintings, drawings and engravings in order to place the furniture in the identical position to when the Duke was alive. She made a near match of the paper – supplied by Clarabut's ('General Draper and Complete House Furnishers') of Deal and commissioned a carpet reproduced from a fragment found at Apsley House. English Heritage recently replaced the original curtains in Wellington's vivid colour scheme – yellow moreen lined with red tammy.

*

The Duke's Room has always been a place of veneration – even without the furniture – although it was once used as a nursery. Another time it was turned into a spare bedroom but only when the castle was overcrowded with house-guests during the residency of Lord Dufferin.

One honoured guest, Sir Donald Mackenzie Wallace, was prevailed upon to sleep in the Duke's Room. Fearing ghosts, his mind worked overtime and his imagination conjured up all kinds of spectres: '. . . in the middle of the night I was disturbed by curious sounds which suggested to my sleepy mind that the shade of the departed did not approve of my presence in the sacred chamber. At last I struck a light and solved the mystery. A thunderstorm was going on and the rain was coming down in torrents on the roof, while at the foot of my bed a little cascade was falling from the ceiling on to a cane-bottomed chair.'

*

The title, 'Wellington', is taken from the manor of Wellington in Somerset which was awarded to the Duke by the nation in 1812. Today the Duke of Wellington is still widely commemorated throughout the world. The capital city of New Zealand – Wellington – was named in honour of him. Also called Wellington are: a mountain in Tasmania; a lake in Australia; a town in Canada; an island off Chile. Numerous warships perpetuated his name as indeed did two RAF bombers, *Wellesley* and *Wellington,* during the Second World War. *Iron*

Duke (Britannia class Pacific No. 70014) was the reserve locomotive employed to haul the Golden Arrow Pullman express service between Victoria and Dover Marine Stations in the 1950s while the mainline station on London's South Bank opened in 1848 still parades the glorious name of Waterloo.

Mundane articles which carried the Duke's portrait to endorse their quality ranged from clay pipes to knife polish, gramophone needles to sandpaper – and even banknotes! A wide variety of plants also propagate his name – a blackcurrant, a tulip, an apple, a rose and a species of tree (Wellingtonia) – which is strange since the Duke remained steadfastly ignorant of horticulture.

It is even more odd to learn than the Duke influenced fashion! Yet there were 'Wellington coats' ('a kind of half-and-half great coat and under-coat meeting close and square below the knees'), 'Wellington trousers' and, of course, the famous 'Wellington boots'.

In Deal and Walmer there still exists an abundance of streets and houses which recall the town's most famous resident. Wellington Parade, along the beach near Kingsdown, recalls the Duke's favourite walk; Wellington House, opposite Victoria Park, marks the site of a once prosperous corn mill while the Lord Warden public house displays a splendid portrait of the Duke and his flag.

*

'Wellington' (registered trade mark) gramophone needle case
(Author's collection)

130

An important collection of Wellingtonia is housed at Walmer Castle. The Lucas collection of memorabilia was collected by Wing-Commander Thomas Hill Lucas (1895 – 1975) and highlights the public side of this soldier-statesman. Wellington's military career peaked after Waterloo and, as his fame spread across Europe, his portrait was in great demand by a hero-worshipping public. When he entered politics he remained in the public eye through engravers and caricaturists. Objects on display illustrate the great and enduring popularity of the Duke throughout the Victorian period and include Staffordshire figures, Parian ware, Toby jugs and portrait busts. Humbler objects number teapots, pot lids, paperweights and even doorstoppers, all stamped with that unmistakable profile. Two wall cabinets exhibit coins and medals celebrating different aspects of his life.

The Wellington Museum, created by Lady Reading, now occupies the apartment popularly called the Duke's Dressing Room. (During his lifetime it was actually a bedroom occupied by the Duke's parliamentary colleague, Charles Arbuthnot.) Important exhibits focus on the private life of the Iron Duke.

Among the artefacts are Wellington's black Wedgewood tea and coffee services; a set of knitting needles in a long case owned by his Duchess and a representation of the Duke's country house, Stratfield Saye, composed of 2,500 tiny pieces of wood made by his estate carpenter for the Great Exhibition of 1851. (This marquetry picture was a favourite piece of the Duke and it hung prominently in a recess in his dining room.)

Personal relics include a pair of fans with intricately carved ivory handles in Chinese style; a telescope in a leather case and an enormous tin candle lantern – all used by the Duke on various campaigns. His dress uniform as Field Marshal is displayed – a scarlet coat with blue collar and cuffs.

There is also the navy blue tailcoat with its crimson collar and cuffs and gleaming brass buttons worn by the Duke when Lord Warden of the Cinque Ports – purchased by Captain Watts immediately after Wellington's death.

Finally, there is a pair of the famous Wellington boots – high boots covering the knees in front and cut away behind – designed by the Duke for his horse- or foot-soldiers on the battlefield. Today they are perhaps the most evocative memento of our most famous LORD WARDEN OF THE CINQUE PORTS.

The Union Jack at half-mast

THE WARDEN OF THE CINQUE PORTS.

A mist was driving down the British Channel,
    The day was just begun,
And through the window-panes, on floor and panel,
    Streamed the red autumn sun.

It glanced on flowing flag and rippling pennon,
    And the white sails of ships;
And, from the frowning rampart, the black cannon
    Hailed it with feverish lips.

Sandwich and Romney, Hastings, Hythe and Dover
    Were all alert that day,
To see the French war-steamers speeding over,
    When the fog cleared away.

Sullen and silent, and like couchant lions,
    Their cannon through the night,
Holding their breath, had watched, in grim defiance,
    The sea-coast opposite.

And now they roared at drum-beat from their stations
    On every citadel;
Each answering each, with morning salutations,
    That all was well.

And down the coast, all taking up the burden,
    Replied the distant forts,
As if to summon from his sleep the Warden
    And Lord of the Cinque Ports.

Him shall no sunshine from the fields of azure,
    No drum-beat from the wall,
No morning gun from the black fort's embrasure,
    Awaken with its call!

No more surveying with an eye impartial
   The long line of the coast,
Shall the gaunt figure of the old Field Marshal
   Be seen upon his post!

For in the night, unseen, a single warrior,
   In sombre harness mailed,
Dreaded of man, and surnamed the Destroyer,
   The rampart wall had scaled.

He passed into the chamber of the sleeper,
   The dark and silent room,
And as he entered, darker grew, and deeper,
   The silence and the gloom.

He did not pause to parley or dissemble,
   But smote the Warden hoar;
Ah! what a blow! that made all England tremble,
   And groan from shore to shore.

Meanwhile, without, the surly cannon waited,
   The sun rose bright o'erhead;
Nothing in Nature's aspect intimated
   That a great man was dead.

Henry Longfellow

Walmer Castle from the sea

134

CAPTAINS OF THE THREE CASTLES

DURING THE DUKE OF WELLINGTON'S RESIDENCY AT WALMER.

WALMER CASTLE

1829-1833   George John Piercy Leith. He had been captain since 1800 but was re-appointed by the Duke.

1833-1857   John James Watts. He was personally appointed by the Duke and was described as 'late captain 85 Foot'. He was the last captain.

DEAL CASTLE

1829-1838   Robert, first Lord Carrington. He had been appointed previously by William Pitt and was re-appointed by the Duke.

1838-1842   William Wellesley-Pole, third Earl of Mornington and Lord Maryborough. He was Wellington's elder brother.

1843-1847   James Andrew Brown Ramsay, Earl (and subsequently Marquis) of Dalhousie, K.T. He resigned in 1847 when he was appointed Governor-General of India. He succeeded Wellington as Lord Warden.

1847-1879   Richard Charles Meade, Earl of Clanwilliam.

SANDOWN CASTLE

1829-1834   John Methurst Poynter. He had been re-appointed by Wellington.

1835-1841	Peter Fisher. Resigned when he was appointed to Sheerness Dockyard.
1844-1848	Edward Harvey. (Afterwards Sir Edward Harvey, G.C.B.) Resigned when he was appointed to Malta Dockyard. He was then Rear Admiral and second in command of the Mediterranean Fleet.
1848-1851	William Wilmot Henderson. Resigned when he was appointed to chief command of south-east coast of South America being then a Rear Admiral.
1851-1855	Sir John Hill, Kt, Rear Admiral of the White. The last captain.

BIBLIOGRAPHY

Wellington in Civil Life – Muriel Wellesley. 1939.
Life of Arthur, Duke of Wellington – G. R. Gleig. 1889.
Life of Benjamin Robert Haydon (Volume III) – Tom Taylor. 1853.
Three Years with Wellington in Private Life by an Ex-Aide de Camp – Lord William Pitt Lennox (Second Edition). 1853.
Words on Wellington – Sir William Fraser, Bt. 1900.
Personal Reminiscences of the Duke of Wellington – Francis, first Earl of Ellesmere (edited by Alice, Countess of Strafford). 1903.
Wellington: The Years of the Sword – Elizabeth Longford. 1969.
Wellington: Pillar of State – Elizabeth Longford. 1972.
A Boy in the Peninsular War, Autobiography of Robert Blakeney, 28 Regiment of Foot – Edited by John Sturgis. 1899.
Adventures in the Rifle Brigade – Captain John Kincaid, 1830.
Conversations with the Duke of Wellington, 1831-1851 – Earl Stanhope. 1888.
Journal of Thomas Raikes, 1831-1847 (4 volumes). 1856.
Journal of Mrs Arbuthnot (Volume 2), 1826-1832 – Edited by Francis Bamford and the Duke of Wellington. 1950.
Journal of Lady Nugent, 1801-1815 – edited by Philip Wright. 1966.
The Wellington Memorial: His Comrades and Contemporaries – Major Arthur Griffiths. 1897.
Life of Queen Victoria – Sarah Tytler. 1902.
Queen Victoria – Giles St Aubyn. 1991.
History of Deal – John Laker. 1917.
History of Deal – Stephen Pritchard. 1864.
Military Life of Field Marshal the Duke of Wellington (Volume I) – Jackson and Scott. 1840.
Life of Wellington (Volume I) – Revd G. N. Wright. 1841.
A Soldier's Wife: Wellington's Marriage – Joan Wilson. 1987.
Correspondence of Sarah, Lady Lyttleton – Edited by Hon. Mrs Hugh Wyndham. 1912.
Life of Wellington (Volumes I-IV) – Williams.
Memoir of Field Marshal the Duke of Wellington (Volume II).
The Duke of Wellington – J. Walter Buchan. 1914.
Wellington and his Friends: Letters of the First Duke Edited by the seventh Duke of Wellington. 1965.

Life of Wellington – George Eliot. 1816.

The Duke – Philip Guedalla. 1931

Annals of Dover – John Bavington Jones. 1916.

Discovering Deal – Barbara Collins. 1969.

Wellington the Beau – Patrick Delaforce. 1990.

A Great Man's Friendship: Letters of the Duke of Wellington to Mary, Marchioness of Salisbury, 1850-1852 – Edited by Lady Burghclere. 1927.

Life of Arthur, Duke of Wellington – Charles Duke Yonge. 1892.

A Memoir of the Duke of Wellington – Charles MacFarlane (with a concluding chapter by T. A. Buckley. A.M.). 1858.

Wellington – John Timbs. 1852.

Memorials of the Goodwin Sands – G. Byng Gattie. 1890.

Goodwin Sands Shipwrecks – Richard Larn. 1977.

Records of Walmer – Revd. C. Elvin. 1890.

Walmer and Walmer Castle – Revd C. Elvin. 1897.

Wellington after Waterloo – Neville Thompson. 1896.

Wellington – F. Tickner. 1941.

An Anecdotal Memoir of Her Royal Highness, the Princess Royal of England – by a Lady. 1858.

The Personal History of Walmer Castle and its Lords Warden – Marquess Curzon of Kedlestone. 1927.

Lifelines 26: Wellington – Amoret and Christopher Scott. 1973.

The Duke of Wellington in Caricature – John Physick. 1965.

Life of Wellington (Volume I) – Sir James Edward Alexander. 1939.

Correspondence of Lady Burghersh with the Duke of Wellington – Edited by Lady Rose Weighall. 1903.

Rural Rides – William Cobbett. 1830.

Railway Carriages in the British Isles – Hamilton Ellis. 1965.

Boat Trains and Channel Packets – Rixon Bucknall. 1957.

Letters of Charles Dickens: 1850-1852. Pilgrim Edition. (Volume VI) – Clarendon Press. 1988.

Walmer Castle and Gardens – J. G. Coad and G. E. Hughes. 1992.

Apsley House – Simon Jervis and Maurice Tomlin. 1984.

The Illustrated London News.

Bygone Kent.

Victoria and Albert – Richard Hough. 1996.

The Heraldry of the Cinque Ports – Geoffrey Williams. 1971.

Rambling Recollections of the Neighbourhood of Dover – 1848.

Dictionary of National Biography.

The Times.

Dover Telegraph and Cinque Ports Advertiser.

Colourful Characters of Dover – Shirley Harrison. 1991.

CREDITS

Photographs of Queen Victoria's locket, the Duke's telescope and the sketch of Wellington by Benjamin Haydon are reproduced by kind permission of His Grace the Duke of Wellington, KG, Stratfield Saye House, Hampshire.

Permission to use original letters of the first Duke of Wellington was granted by Lady Morrison and the Trustees of the Madresfield Estate, Worcestershire, and the Hulke medical papers were made available by English Heritage.

Special photography for reproduction in this book was taken by Paul Andrew, Head of Photography at South Kent College.

For specialist advice regarding Wellington's life and career I am indebted to:

Mr Patrick Aubrey-Fletcher, ARICS, Comptroller, Stratfield Saye House;
Mr Peter Beal, Department of Printed Books and Manuscripts, Sotheby's;
Mrs Sonia Berry;
Mrs Sarah Campbell, former curator of Dover Museum;
Mrs Judith Doré;
Mr Mark Frost;
Mr Ian Giles;
Revd Gary Gill;
Revd Peter Hammond, former vicar of Old and New St Mary's Church, Walmer;
Revd Bruce Hawkins, vicar of Old and New St Mary's Church, Walmer;
Mr Ken Horne;
Mr Sydney Hulke;
Mr Jonathan Kinghorn, Senior Regional Curator, English Heritage;
Ms Jenifer Miller, Administrator, the Wellington Museum, Apsley House;
The National Railway Museum, York;
The Print Room, Deal;
Mr Alan Parnell, former Custodian, Walmer Castle;
Mr A. W. Potter, Information Assistant, The Royal Academy of Arts;
Mr Derek Saunders, Curator, The Waterloo Museum, Broadstairs;
Mr Ron Sullivan, Deputy Director, the West India Committee;

Mr John Skelton;
Mr Malcolm Swan, Acting Head Custodian, Walmer Castle;
The Late Mr John Turner of the Deal Society;
The Victoria and Albert Museum;
Miss Christine Waterman, B.A., Curator, Dover Museum;
Mr Tony Watford;
Mr Alan S. Watts, President of the Dickens' Fellowship;
Dorothy Williams, Archivist, Madresfield Court;
Mrs Joan Wilson, former Archivist, Stratfield Saye;
Mr J. Joseph Wisdom, M.A., Librarian, St Paul's Cathedral;
Mr Francis Wright.

Wellington to Lady Salisbury while wandering
through the woods at Walmer in 1836:

'I feel I am but a man.'

Dover Castle in Victorian times